THE COLONIAL SIGNS OF
INTERNATIONAL RELATIONS

HIMADEEP MUPPIDI

The Colonial Signs of International Relations

Columbia University Press
New York

Columbia University Press
Publishers Since 1893
New York
cup.columbia.edu
© Himadeep Muppidi, 2012

Library of Congress Cataloging-in-Publication Data

Muppidi, Himadeep.
  The colonial signs of international relations / Himadeep Muppidi.
      p. cm.
  Includes bibliographical references and index.
  ISBN: 978-0-231-70122-8 (cloth : alk. paper)
          978-0-231-80108-9 (e-book)
  1. International relations. 2. Imperialism. I. Title.

  JZ1242.M85 2012
  325'.3—dc23

                        2011047475

∞

Columbia University Press books are printed on permanent and
durable acid-free paper. This book is printed on paper with recycled
content.
Printed in India

c 10 9 8 7 6 5 4 3 2 1

For
Ishika and Dhruv

Crises in World Politics
(Centre of International Studies, University of Cambridge)

TARAK BARKAWI • JAMES MAYALL • BRENDAN SIMMS
editors

GÉRARD PRUNIER
Darfur: the Ambiguous Genocide

MARK ETHERINGTON
Revolt on the Tigris

FAISAL DEVJI
Landscapes of the Jihad

AHMED HASHIM
Insurgency and Counter-Insurgency in Iraq

ERIC HERRING & GLEN RANGWALA
Iraq in Fragments: the Occupation and its Legacy

STEVE TATHAM
Losing Arab Hearts and Minds

WILLIAM MALEY
Rescuing Afghanistan

IAIN KING AND WHIT MASON
Peace at any Price: How the World Failed Kosovo

CARNE ROSS
Independent Diplomat

FAISAL DEVJI
*The Terrorist in Search of Humanity: Militant Islam
and Global Politics*

JOHN BEW, MARTYN FRAMPTON & IÑIGO GURRUCHAGA
*Talking to Terrorists: Making Peace in Northern Ireland and the
Basque Country*

HANS KUNDNANI
*Utopia or Auschwitz: Germany's 1968 Generation
and the Holocaust*

AMRITA NARLIKAR
New Powers: How to Become One and How to Manage Them

HIMADEEP MUPPIDI
The Colonial Signs of International Relations

CONTENTS

ACKNOWLEDGEMENTS

This text has been a long time in the making and has passed through the hands of friends, colleagues, students, teachers and family. Their touch has, in molding its meanings or honing its texture, improved it considerably. Memory being fickle and my record-keeping poor, my apologies in advance if I have failed to explicitly acknowledge all those who have helped. I am solely responsible, however, for all the flaws that remain in the text.

In writing this book, I have been fortunate enough to be part of a learning community nurtured in/by a number of places. This community sustains me intellectually and socio-emotionally. Although too large to name here, some aspects of this community are condensed around institutions. At Vassar College, I am happy to have the friendship and profound engagement of Andy Bush, Andy Davison, Khadija El-Alaoui, Luke Harris, Katie Hite, Bill Hoynes, Joe Nevins and superbly thoughtful colleagues in the Department of Political Science as well as the programs in International Studies and Asian Studies. I am also lucky to have the opportunity to learn constantly, in class and outside, from deeply thoughtful and intensely idealistic Vassar students. Particularly noteworthy in recent years are those who have created and sustained "The Village" at Vassar and beyond. Villages, by their very nature, resist naming but from within that warmly hospitable space Jason Vargas, Kelly Tan, Thomas Facchine, Túlio Zille and Quỳnh Phạm

ACKNOWLEDGEMENTS

read, re-read, *adda-ed*, raised questions, commented or criticized various issues developed in these chapters. I am thankful for their friendship and their generously critical spirit.

In the time that this manuscript has taken to emerge into print, earlier versions of two chapters ("Shame and Rage" and "Zoological Relations") have appeared in *Interrogating Imperialism* edited by Naeem Inayatullah and Robin Riley (Palgrave-Macmillan, UK, 2006) and *Europe and its Boundaries* edited by Andrew Davison and Himadeep Muppidi (Lexington Press, US, 2009) respectively. Parts of this book have also been presented and discussed at various venues over the years including the "Bud Fest" in Minneapolis, the Minnesota International Relations Colloquium at the University of Minnesota, Temple University, Jawaharlal Nehru University (JNU) and the Annual Conventions of the International Studies Association. I would like to thank the editors and publishers of the two edited books as well as the discussants and participants in the various fora for their suggestions, perceptive readings, advice and criticisms. Specific thanks are owed to Bud Duvall, Alex Wendt, Roxanne Doty, Michael Barnett, Tarak Barkawi, Rhona Liebel, Janice Bially Mattern, Priya Joshi, Orfeo Fioretos, Latha Varadarajan, Shampa Biswas, Arjun Chowdhury, Mark Hoffman and David Pak Leon.

Bud Duvall remains an inspiring icon for me in many ways. His sharp analyses and insightful readings have always been a pleasure to receive and/or observe and learn from. I am thoroughly in his debt for many richly layered conversations over the years and very specifically for his generous willingness to allow our co-authored piece on humanitarianism (part of a larger co-authored critique of Humanitarianism) to be included here.

Tarak Barkawi was kind enough to rescue the manuscript from cold storage at a University Press and resuscitate it for the series he edits at Hurst. I am grateful to him and to Michael Dwyer for their relatively quick turn-around of this manuscript. Tarak, Michael and David Blaney also reviewed the manuscript and suggested changes (including, among others, doubling the size of the original manuscript!) that, while increasing the time required for revisions, also improved it considerably. David Blaney has, for a long time, been an excellent interlocutor in a number of ways and one of the few joys of a Minnesota winter is getting to a warm cup of coffee and a heated conversation with David on Grand Avenue. I am also deeply appreciative of Jonathan de Peyer's careful reading and meticulous editing of the manuscript as it was being prepared for publication.

Janice Bially Mattern proposed the book for discussion at the ISA-North East's Annual Book Circle. A very formidable group, including Janice, Linda Bishai, Robin Riley, Rose Shinko, Peter Mandaville and Naeem Inayatullah dissected the book in ways that were inspiring, provocative and immensely useful for further revision. I have also been fortunate to receive advice, criticism and suggestions for further improvement on various chapters from Jenny Edkins, Cynthia Enloe, Poornima Paidipaty, Kiran Pervez and Naren Kumarakulasingam as well as those who reviewed this manuscript as external reviewers of my tenure file at Vassar. Many thanks to you all!

In India, over the years, I have learnt from a continuing and intensely critical engagement with Rajesh Rajagopalan, Gaddam Dharmendra, Udita Chandra, Kashyap Kumar, Manoj Mitta, Bala Venkatesh Varma, Rajeswari Pillai Rajagopalan, B.S. Chimni, C.S.R. Murthy, and Siddharth Mallavarapu. The prospect of meeting them turns chaotic Delhi into an appealing haven. Biju Mathew, Sangeeta Kamat, Rama Mantena, Kavita Datla, Velcheru Narayana Rao, Sundeep Muppidi, Anant Maringanti, Amar Muppidi, K. Srinivas

Reddy, Anjana Sinha, Ladan Affi and Vinod Menon are part of a larger, vibrant community that informs, invigorates and criticizes me regularly. I am deeply appreciative of that privilege.

Naeem Inayatullah set me on the path of an alternative International Relations (IR) through a number of conversations and continually inspires me to push intellectual-emotional boundaries within and without. Nothing gives me greater pleasure than snagging every opportunity to engage him at the ISA or anywhere else I can get to embrace him. I am not sure what really happens in these encounters but the outcome is almost always an enhancement of my own thinking-being in IR and the world! Directly and indirectly, this text is a tribute to his brilliant capacity to ignite subaltern othernesses within our selves.

Chris Chekuri and Quỳnh Phạm are the two souls I talk to endlessly. It is one of the exquisite pleasures of academic life that these conversations constitute work and play. Co-authors in thought as well as in writing, they inspire me to continuously explore, engage and re-articulate the world in new and innovative ways.

My dispersed but techno-socially knit family continues to sustain me in many ways. I regret that my father, who passed away in December 2009, did not live to see this book in print. But he opened my mind first to the world of international relations and his adventurous and bold spirit continues to bless and guide me as I fumble around fascinated and bewildered by its intricacies! My mother's intelligence, calm strength and fiery resoluteness have always inspired me to think deeper about the multiple sources of social power in our seemingly singular world. I am forever indebted to both of them for teaching me, primarily through the force of example, what living a dignified and meaningful life entails. As my children Ishika and Dhruv ask me about international relations, I hope this book tells them what it is but should not be. As to what it ought to be, I believe they as well as Kruthin, Siri, Keerthi, Saif, Gabriel, Yamina and Leo, will be in a far better position to script that.

"...death has a bad odor that cannot be smelled except by those who are going through its agony..."[1]

INTRODUCTION

Death stinks. Left unattended, it finds many ways to make its presence felt. Jogging on the college grounds, it is not unusual to be suddenly assailed by the stench of a dead animal in the bushes. I take notice, maybe make a passing comment to my jogging companion, and continue running.

I imagine dead humans stink too. I say imagine because, unlike the stench of dead animals, or of rotting potatoes, or of slimy mushrooms, I cannot recall any strong sensory evidence of that stench. I do remember being emotionally and physically in the company of dead human beings, generally relatives or friends, have visual sketches of some of these deaths, have felt death's coldness skin to skin, but as a stench, as an assailing of my nose, I have little or no memory of its presence. I haven't ever really smelt dead human beings. But I suspect I shouldn't have too much trouble imagining that stench, especially given the nature of what I study: international relations.

International relations is a field littered with dead and dying bodies. But the dead never seem to rot or stink, whether portrayed discreetly or starkly, sketched crudely or stylistically. Qana, Haditha, Fallujah. International relations overflows with corpses. I see them every day. Trained primarily to conceptualize some piles of corpses as a sign of "power" and others as "crimes against humanity," other languages of the body pass me by silently.

Day in and day out, a few rituals have marked the past few summers for me. I fire up the browser, and check out the *New York Times*, the *Washington Post*, *The Hindu*, and *AsiaTimes*. Naked bodies, thin, cold and hungry, crowd the periphery and center of my reading trails but my eyes skip as lightly over the ads either side, as they do over the dead center-square. When, occasionally, my eyes stumble over a corpse, I pause, maybe in order to feel something befitting this sight. I wait a few seconds, presuming that something will emerge from within, something that I assume will be an appropriate emotional response to the deaths of others, something that will allow me to go on. Dead Iraqis, dead Shiites, dead Sunnis, dead Palestinians, dead Afghans, dead Mumbaikars, dead Kashmiris: what do I owe them? Don't I owe them a moment's silence as I step over them in search of the international? But nothing appropriate is forthcoming. I can only think: what sort of theory of international relations (IR) can arrest or grasp these deaths, do justice to these piles of human dead?

Occasionally, an image or audio clip lingers. The picture of a boy, in Tyre, Lebanon, dressed in red, with a bloodied face and a look of incomprehension; his mother, also bloodied, in black, on her back but reaching out to him as if to explain what had transformed their world so suddenly, so horribly. An item in the *New York Times* about children killed in Qana juxtaposed with a headline about letting American children be children in kindergarten. Audio fragments over NPR about the killing of a young Iraqi girl by Marines. As I catch the last story, in between dropping my kids in Kindercare, one of the reporters keeps using the word "female"—"the Iraqi female"—in talking about the assaulted and murdered girl because, as he explains it, there is some dispute about her age. His obsessive precision jars, though I cannot pinpoint exactly why. Is it because his fastidiousness is a distraction from the horrifying nature of the event? Does it remind me too much of my disciplinary protocols that also value precision over feelings? Or, is it because the reporter, in his insistence on capturing her essence, is repeating the crime again and again?

"He looked like a hunted fox," said an eye-witness to a shooting in a London subway. Another audio fragment from NPR (or was it the BBC?) sticks in the mind, about a Brazilian who was chased and shot because the police mistakenly identified him as a terrorist. Foxes, females and children thus linger visually, disturbingly, aurally, but as dead bodies, as corpses—they don't stink. Crispness dominates the newsprint. Fresh air abounds on the radio waves; rigor and precision define theory in IR. But the stuffiness of dead bodies, their unpleasing decomposition, their stench, rarely comes through our fields.

But corpses do stink, don't they? Bodies putrefy in death. Living tissue turns rotten. And when such things happen on a mass scale in international relations, shouldn't our theories catch, convey and account for that stench? How have we managed to avoid that?

Shashi Tharoor, writer, diplomat, Member of the Indian Parliament, narrates an insightful and relevant story about Truth:

> It seems that in ancient times a brash young warrior sought the hand of a beautiful princess. The king, her father, thought the warrior was a bit too cocksure and callow; he told him he could only marry the princess once he had found Truth. So the young warrior set out on a quest for Truth. He went to temples and to monasteries, to mountaintops where sages meditated and to forests where ascetics scourged themselves, but nowhere could he find Truth.
>
> Despairing one day and seeking refuge from a thunderstorm, he found himself in a dank, musty cave. There, in the darkness, was an old hag, with warts on her face and matted hair, her skin hanging in folds from her bony limbs, her teeth broken, her

breath malodorous. She greeted him; she seemed to know what he was looking for. They talked all night, and with each word she spoke, the warrior realised he had come to the end of his quest. She was Truth. In the morning, when the storm broke, the warrior prepared to return to claim his bride. "Now that I have found Truth," he said, "what shall I tell them at the palace about you?" The wizened old crone smiled. "Tell them," she said, "tell them that I am young and beautiful."[2]

Ugly though it might be, Truth desires to be presented as young and beautiful. Does a similar desire—the aesthetics of rigor, precision and objectivity—haunt IR? Realists pride themselves on their unflinching embrace of ugly Truths. Is there, in those stoic embraces, a peculiar romance, a romance with the heroism of the self? If not, how do we understand that their brave passions for truth only seem to deliver instrumental and amoral actions towards others? Do they forget that the warrior and the "old hag" "talked all night" and that "with each word she spoke, the warrior realized he had come to the end of his quest"? Liberals believe that "the old hag's" ugliness is superficial, that underneath the warts is a "young and beautiful" girl and that all we need to do is to clean her up a bit; touch her up in our image. The self-consciously more critical among IR theorists quarrel with the universalizing claims of the realists and liberals and point to the racial, gender and regional specificity of "hags" (Is she American? Western? European?) But do we do so only to prepare the stage for our young and beautiful Ms. Universe (Asian, African, Latin American, Third World, Non-Western) to come into the light? Would we dare deny our Truth its youth and beauty? Could we imagine that our Truth, when discovered in some dank cave, might very well be ugly and yet be a compelling conversationalist (as well as a smiling liar)?

The stench and specter of ugliness! Truths that are not attractive, despite their self-presentation, and do not draw us to them by a promise of visual, aural or visceral pleasure. Mouths that are malodorous with teeth that are broken, jagged, uneven; bodies whose skin falls off the bones and whose hair is matted. Bodies that smell when alive and stink when dead, but bodies that greet you and always already talk compellingly.

What would it mean for IR to converse with such bodies? What self-referential and sole/soul-pleasuring fantasies of power, beauty and excitement about world politics and the nature of knowledge must we relinquish for such conversations to occur, for the smell of bodies to permeate and be part of our understandings? What body languages do we need to be literate about?

Having encountered Truth as an ugly but compelling conversationalist and a likely liar on occasion, what responsibility befalls the warrior? How should he translate his conversations with Truth? Is it the King, the Palace and the Princess that he should keep uppermost in his mind since it was their interests that he set out to please and win over initially? Should he be faithful to his conversational partner's ability to reveal the world to him or to her wily desire to represent herself otherwise? Unsure about interests, ambiguous about fidelities, and convinced that not every ugliness I encounter is a form of truth, I'll focus, in the pages that follow, on the conflicting responses of the self. What ensues are conversations with ugliness—theirs and ours; here and there—and the subterranean relations of responsibility that such engagements can reveal. These are relations not just of power and interest but also of shame and rage, of a scandalous numbness to mass death, of outrageous proprieties in the face of atrocities and of cognitive complicities in the zoological productions of fellow others. These are my/our international relations.

* * *

Colonialism is, I believe, one such ugly experience of international relations. While historically the experience of colonialism has been a traumatic one[3] for many people, its modern understanding in international relations appears to lack any memory of its pain and its horror. Contemporary theorists of the international translate/conceptualize colonialism primarily as an asymmetry of state power and governance involving gains and losses, and concerns about racist attitudes. Subtracting the racism and governing correctly, it follows from their arguments, might actually make colonialism a desirable model of governance for our times. Postcolonial theorists have yet to properly counter such translations effectively. Following the insights of Jenny Edkins,[4] this book seeks to take preliminary steps in that direction by marking the traumatic nature of colonialism and in doing so re-opening multiple "layers of possibility" and the larger spaces of the political in international relations that are foreclosed by such translations.

Organizing Principles

I begin with a chapter that explores the feelings of shame and rage that arise within me as I look at some recent and not so recent events in international relations. This leads me to argue for an IR that is anti-colonial rather than simply post-colonial. While agreeing with Dipesh Chakrabarty[5] that the possibility of an anti-colonial social theory/IR necessitates the "provincialization" (self and otherwise) of "Europe," what comes in the way of this provincialization is the constant generation of narratives of the international, even in their more progressive forms, that locate universal norms within a shifting but central "hyperreal Europe." The presence and pervasiveness of atrocities in the history of Europe does little to upset such narratives. Even in those circumstances where the committing of an atrocity can be attributed solely to Europe, narratives of the international effectively reverse the role of perpetrator and per-petrated. Seeking to make sense of this, I delve into the proto-cols governing the narration of atrocities in international relations. These are protocols that consistently structure the cognition and representation of non-Europeans through a zoo-logical modality while writing the self in the role of the zoo-keeper. Such protocols cannot help but produce a complicity of the post-colonial self when it seeks to be proper only in its nar-rations and translations of the international. We need to find ways of addressing and talking to zookeepers that transgress their expectations of animals. Following the insights generated by theorists working on the politics of translations, what this entails is the need to focus on the production of translations that are scandalous.

The chapters in the book are structured according to this unifying theme. Beginning with an exploration of feelings of shame and rage (Chapter 1), I discuss the proprieties of IR as they pertain to narratives of mass destruction and of colonial atrocities (Chapters 2 and 3). I explore such narratives to extract the protocols governing the writing of the European Self and non-European Other in IR/IPE and to highlight the zoological modalities and complicities that are implicated in recognizing the Other (Chapters 4–7). I conclude with a focus on the politics of translation that can transgress these different forms of colonial protocols scandalously.

1

SHAME AND RAGE[1]

I

Splayed objects of your worldly gaze
Captive loves of your studies abroad
Slaves, sepoys, spices
Animal specimens, software-species
Unequally sold
Civilly exchanged
Off-shored, shackled, tortured
Out-sourced
In otherwise humane designs
Are we burning, freezing, coding, bleeding
Disappearing in History
As you hum-vee and bull-doze
The *Wadi al-Uyouns* of our Life[2]

II

Bodies, Brown and Naked

A friend emails me photographs from Abu Ghraib. I had
already seen some of them. These I hadn't. The brief glimpse

of the new ones roils my stomach. Disturbed, I shut down the computer. I want to erase those images from my hard drive; unpool their film from my eyes. I feel debased and complicit merely by looking. I want to retreat, run, from the implication in those pictures. I am possessed, simultaneously, by a desire to prove them false. They must have been staged, must be untrue, I think. I consider scanning the images closely to comfort myself in that confirmation. But I don't find the courage to look again. Then I wonder if the "truth" of these images was really the issue here. These photographs were alive and moving. They had already traveled from the Middle East to the Northeast. And it was the Bush administration that had charged these pictures with plausibility even as it had electrocuted the lives of many others.

Colleagues I respect are puzzled by my response to the photographs: "What," they inquire politely but with just that correct touch of annoyed incredulity, "did you imagine happens in war?" I don't begrudge them that annoyance: What *did* I imagine happened in war? Why was I, who so routinely preach the power of language, finding it so difficult to grasp what a language of power and war necessarily entailed? Deep down, did I continue to think that war was only "politics by other means"? Did the qualifier "only" allow me to hide from myself what the otherness of the means implied? Did I think of war as primarily a technical relationship that, addressed properly, could be clean, cleansing and cultured? Was it then basically the nakedness of the Other in Abu Ghraib that was bothering me? Was their difficult-to-hide brownness cutting too close to my bone?

In the first Gulf War, the United States bulldozed Iraqi soldiers into the sand in order to bury the ghosts of Vietnam. In the second Gulf War, it wanted to awe the world by tearing apart and suturing twenty-five million people. But each encounter in the invasion/occupation/liberation of Iraq by the US only serves to galvanize the scarcely rested specters of colonialism. Every uncounted corpse, every unaccounted for death, every blasted body, revivifies memories and energizes the images of those slashed, burnt, buried, bombed and napalmed in Vietnam, in the Philippines, in Iran, in Iraq, in Cuba, in the Americas. If this is what the US can do in the face of global disapproval and in the name of good intentions, then what has it done when neither the mask of humanity nor the avowal of a good intention was a necessary feature of world politics? What other ghosts wait to be resurrected here?

I am reminded of Belgium's invasion/occupation/liberation of the Congo in order, ostensibly, to save it from Arab slavers. That liberation, that missionary politics by means of the Other, crucified millions of Africans and had its own Abu Ghraibs: photographs of shackled, naked African women held in chains to coerce their husbands to gather rubber for the Belgians; pictures of the limbs of children and men—hands and feet chopped off by the militia of the Anglo-Belgian India Rubber Company; photo-portraits of Belgian officers posing nobly—the archives bristle with these images.[3] Moonlighting as authors, artists, painters and collectors even as they were looting and killing, officers such as Leon Rom gaze into the future as if convinced of the grandness of their enterprise, the pedagogical necessity of their violence and the nobility of their civilization. There is little in Mr. Rom's photo-portrait to signal us that this member of the Entomological Society of Belgium—every time he returned to Europe he brought back many specimens of butterflies—was also renowned for collecting and displaying, in his Congolese garden, rows of severed African heads.[4] An officer, an entomologist, and a head-hunter—cultured to the core.

But that, you might say, as the Belgians now do, was another time.

Some decades later, we see photo- or video-graphic beheadings as signs of the backward, brutal Other. Made over by modernity, we talk tastefully of bombing human communities in and out of time ("into the stone age"), savor festive spectacles of mass killing ("shock and awe") and marvel at the radiant and precise aesthetics of Predators, depleted Uranium shells, and 500-pound bombs dropped on unsuspecting families suspected of harboring terrorists. So if Abu Ghraib is disquieting, is it only because it hurts my culturally-honed tastes in dispensing coolly and cleanly with the Other? Do I prefer my killers to be like my TV anchors: well-dressed, well-spoken and light of color?

III

The Remains/Returns of the Colonized

The Royal Museum of Central Africa in Tervuren, Belgium, is proud of its collection of objects and animals. That collection includes, on its own authority, 350 archives, 8,000 musical instruments, 20,000 maps, 56,000 wood samples, 180,000 ethnographic objects, 250,000 rock samples and 10,000,000 animals.[5] Notwithstanding a passion for enumeration, the Royal Museum has trouble remembering the number of human beings intimately implicated in this collection. If we distributed the animal collection alone, going by the current population of Belgium, that's nearly an animal specimen each for every living Belgian citizen. But if we counted only those who died to make this rich collection possible—5,000,000 to 8,000,000 Congolese—even a very conservative estimate would mean placing the remains of a murdered African in the hands of every Belgian couple.

14

I went to Brussels in the summer of 2004 after finding out that, nearly a hundred years ago, King Leopold II of Belgium wanted to start a World School of Colonialism.[6] The World School of Colonialism was expected to be part of a larger architectural complex that would include a Museum, a Conference Center and a Sports Complex. Leopold's death in 1909 resulted in only the Royal Museum part of the project being realized. Trained to think of colonialism as an ideology that dissimulates even as it dismembers, I was startled by the nakedness of the King's proposal.

The Royal Museum is designed to impress. Gilded bronze sculptures welcome you into the marble-floored rotunda of the Museum. You look up to see tall Belgian citizens bestowing gifts—the "values" of "civilization," "well-being," "support," and freedom from "slavery"—on Congolese children, women and men. Prophet-like, the demeanor of these benevolent citizens brooks no rude question on the source of the virtues flowing from their hands. A path leads from the rotunda to sections of the Museum showcasing displays marked as anthropology, history, zoology, agricultural and forest economy, geology, prehistory and archeology before arriving back at the entrance.

As I began my tour in anthropology, my eyes started, in a most unscholarly fashion, to glaze over the neatly labeled drums and masks and the many, many figurines. Something seemed amiss, something was out-of-focus in the long cultivated relationship between the eye and the eyed. Try as I might, I couldn't summon the proper academic disposition that this institutional space seemed, quite silently, to demand. The pressure intensified as I became doubly aware of those around me in anthropology. I realized that I was reflecting on their likely reflections of me walking these corridors. Brown imagining White imagining brown eyes seeking traction on black masks.

15

My unease kept mounting until I strolled into the zoology section. Seeing some children clustered around a teacher, I paused hesitantly in my wanderings, wondering whether they might have as many questions of me as of the Okapi. I was not sure I was ready to hear those questions yet. But in zoology I grasped, suddenly and sharply, that my unease was emerging from the underlying design of the museum. Understood as a manifestation of the European order of things, the museum made brilliant sense. Here was the trophy room, laboratory, library, school, hospital and asylum of the colonizer. This was where they—the colonizer's citizen-heirs—repaired to be educated, trained, cultured and restored to/into their patrimony. But what was my place and position in such an institution? Where did I fit in an institution displaying the colonizer's collections? In the European order of things, was I, could I be, only another animal-object?

As long as I was gazing from and moving on the observer-academic side of the glass border, I was a peculiarity in the Museum, an anomaly inviting comment, not least from my own self. This Museum was not built for the likes of me to gaze and move. Just as we don't design zoos to help the animals examine the displays, this Museum was not designed on the premise that the colonized would, one day, be walking through its corridors. Not that there was not a place for those of my tribe. Our assigned place in the Museum's archaeology of knowledge was in natural history, on the observed-Other side of the glass with the dead if absent and unacknowledged Africans and the equally dead but publicly presented and proudly displayed animals. Wedged into natural history, suturing nature and history, wouldn't my normalized identity preclude any straying from the familial intimacy of traditional villages and stuffed elephants?

But crossing these borders, straying beyond my assigned positions, was also the necessary condition of my education here. To walk through the Museum—anomalous as that might have been in terms of its founding principles—was to discover, as intended by King Leopold II, what a colonial education/responsibility was all about.[7] Having grasped colonization from a diligent reading of the archives of the Spanish Conquistadors, Leopold II was no doubt a masterly teacher of the craft.[8] Mobile within Europe, moving amongst the colonizers, at least partly because of a degree in International Relations, I couldn't help wondering if and how my education differed from the one that the King wanted to offer. How certain was I that my degree was not already from an affiliate of the World School of Colonialism?

Trading places, switching gazes, looking in from the observed-Other, eyed side of the glass, I understood now that I was the turbaned slaver, the rag-head, on display, whose "Arabness" was deployed as the motive for Belgium's soul-cleansing antislavery campaigns. But I was also the shackled Congolese, the coolie, animal-slave to Belgium's hunger for rubber and ivory. And universality and humanity, colonial education as well as "real and responsible" international relations were about ceaselessly rescuing one from the Other, the coolie from the rag-head, the animal-slave from the slaver-object, the African from the Arab, the good Muslim from the bad one, the academic-observer from the observed-academic object, me from myself, but without ever setting any of us free.

IV

Interrogating In-Betweenity

If Belgium sees itself as the "heart of Europe," the Grand-Place in Brussels similarly presents itself as one of Europe's most beautiful public squares, and is generally regarded as such. Belgium claimed a place for it on the World Heritage List by asserting that it was "a masterpiece of human creative genius, with a special quality of coherency..." An expert mission from the World Heritage Commission, evaluated Belgium's claims and agreed that it deserved a place on the List for, among other things, the ways in which "the nature...of its architecture" and its "outstanding quality as a public open space," illustrated "in an exceptional way," "the evolution and achievements of a highly successful mercantile city of northern Europe at the height of its prosperity."[9]

An integral part of this most beautiful of European squares, this "masterpiece of human creative genius," this "outstanding public open space," is a building called "Le Roy de l'Espagne." Built by a bakers' guild in 1696–97, this is a "large dignified structure with a balustrade decorated with allegorical statues and surmounted by a graceful dome."[10] Gracing the façade of the "Le Roy de l'Espagne," dignifying it quite prominently, are two captives: a turbaned Moor and a Native American. On their knees, hands bound behind their backs, they are towered over by the crowned head of Charles II.

Diagonally across "Le Roy de l'Espagne," is the bar where Karl Marx and Friedrich Engels are reported to have spent hours polishing the Communist Manifesto. Captivated by this material testimonial to "human creative genius," to the evolution and achievements of Europe, to dignity and grace, I cannot help wondering if Europe's best and brightest citizens, Marx and Engels, gave the captive Moor and the native American some sustained and serious thought. If they had, would they have polished the Manifesto a little further, maybe until it read: "A spectre is ravaging Europe—the spectre of colonialism"? I imagine, uncharitably no doubt, the impatient response of my radical colleagues: "But that's already covered in the section on primitive accumulation. You should read your Marx more carefully."

And maybe I should. But I am straying again, wandering, thinking now of another Charles, of Charles Graner, smiling, posing, thumbs up, behind a pyramid of naked, hooded Iraqi captives in Abu Ghraib. Leaning over this primitive accumulation of brown bodies, smiling again, is another soldier, Meghan Ambuhl. The glee in her eyes, as also the joyful participation in similar rituals of another soldier Pvt. Lyndie England, has been the source of anxious commentary among some feminists: How can historically oppressed subjects participate so pleasurably in the torture and degradation of others?

I understand the participation, maybe not the glee.

I detect no glee in the archival pictures from the Belgian colonization of the Congo.[11] The African soldier guarding two naked, shackled African women is fully clothed, has a gun and is looking at the camera from in between the two hostages. But there is no smile on his face. In another picture, a *chicotte* hovers above a naked African spread-eagled on the ground, face turned away from the camera. The wielder of the *chicotte*, another African, is looking at us, his hand half-raised as if about to strike, but there's little gaiety on his face or in his demeanor. Do these overseers find it difficult to enjoy their violent power because they sense how easily their roles can be reversed with those held hostage or being whipped? Is there no glee in their faces because they know that neither the gun nor the *chicotte* have as much power as pigmentation?

But, crossing borders again, is it precisely a faith in the irreversibility of roles with the darker others, a magical blindness induced by the color of the ostensibly foreign, that allows Marine sergeant Robert Sarra, a veteran of the Iraq war and a peace activist, to shout, in "drunken rage," at a "foreign cabdriver: 'I wiped out your entire family over there, and I'll get you, too?'"[12] As I think of this outburst, I imagine neither terror nor anxiety on the face of the "foreign cabdriver" as he/she hears this. I am sure he/she knows, by now, that in the colonial order of things, they are both substitutable for varied others— "your entire family over there"—and dispensable—"I wiped out your entire family...and I'll get you, too." The cabdriver is calm but shame and rage inundate me as Robert Sarra's drunken words set off a slideshow of my "entire family over there."

Mine is the turbaned head trampled in the Royal Chapel of your Capilla Real de Granada. We circle around the tombs of the Catholic Kings Ferdinand and Isabella. You talk of canonizing Isabella. When I remind you that the conquest of the Americas obliterated much of the Other, you counter by declaring that Isabella, in her will, liberated her Indian slaves.

Mine is the body you cremated twice, thoughtfully: once in Hiroshima and again in Nagasaki. Come anniversary time in August, you are suddenly silent, uncertain about whether to celebrate your technology or atone for the mass vaporizations? But, all year round, you are outraged or terrified that darker rogues might access your destructive wisdom.

Mine is the childishly thin back peeling out from clouds of napalm; mine are the guts spilled out in a million My Lais and squashed in the rubble of bombed Afghan and Iraqi weddings. I lie among the 600 who were sniper-slaughtered to avenge the four dead in Fallujah. I am one of the 208 who are dying every week in Iraq because you wanted "freedom to march" in foreign lands. And the hundreds of thousands more dead that will follow from your murderous and illiterate needs. But even as the rage in me rises, I cannot escape my sense of shame. Shame and rage. You ask me if I want to interrogate imperialism.

I do. But how can I interrogate it without interrogating myself, the postcolonial in-between? If shame and rage are what you-I feel, why do I talk and teach about the indispensability of your thought to my being in the world? Why does the farthest reach of my pedagogy imagine only the possibility of "provincializing" you? Is it because I cannot imagine being Other than what you-I am now: the African with the *chicotte*, the Indian with the gun, the postcolonial with the keyboard? Have I, in the process of post-colonization forgotten what it means to be anticolonial? Or, was anticolonialism never really the aim of my being?

V

A Subaltern West

Teaching Amitav Ghosh's *In an Antique Land*, this semester, I was drawn, once again, to that angry shouting match that Ghosh finally has with the Imam of the village. Needled by the Imam about the "primitive and backward" practices of cow-worship and cremation, Ghosh finds it difficult to restrain himself and lashes out, furiously, about the ways in which India, his country, notwithstanding these practices, outranked the Imam's on the scale of advancement. Since advancement was measured by access to weapons, machines and the means of violence, Ghosh claims superiority on the basis of his country's ability to test nuclear weapons. Even as the exchange winds down, a weary Ghosh is "crushed" further by the thought that this exchange itself—an effort by the representatives of two "superseded civilizations…to establish a prior claim to the technology of modern violence"—was proof of their "final defeat." It was indicative of a world in which the languages of mutual accommodation had been erased by the languages of "guns and tanks and bombs."[13]

Through this distressing conclusion, Ghosh draws a similarity and a difference between himself and the Imam. He points out that this moment of anger and hostility between them was also the moment of perfect understanding since they both realized that they were travelling in the only space that each considered worth travelling—the West. But Ghosh also shadows this moment of identity with the Imam with an apparent difference in their mutual engagement with the West: "The only difference was that I had actually been there, in person: I could have told him a great deal about it, seen at first hand, its libraries, its museums, its theatres..."[14]

Ghosh's assertion of his "first hand" experience of the West's "libraries... museums...theatres" presents the promise, however briefly, of an Other West, a different West, a West that was more than, other than, the possessor of the technologies of modern violence. I say briefly primarily because Ghosh goes on to say that this difference would not have mattered because, for millions of people around the world, this Other West was "mere fluff." I also flag the briefness because much of this book is about the intimate connection between western/colonial processes of knowledge acquisition and the disappearance of a global, cosmopolitan "world of accommodations." But, despite the briefness of its appearance, the promise of an Other West that Ghosh holds out may be worth revisiting. What is intriguing is that he holds out the promise of a subaltern West available for "first-hand experience" in its libraries, museums and theatres.

Contrary to Ghosh's claim, the West's subalternity, if it is to be found, is not necessarily in its "libraries and museums and theatres." Accumulators of knowledge, memory and art, these monopolizing institutions are but sophisticated extensions of the technologies of modern violence. They stand as visible monuments to the West's historical capacity and willingness to freeze, shock, recollect and suture Others. The brazen and easy resurgence of a discourse of empire in the West is evidence that

the educational and cultural machinery of the West offers, primarily, degrees in colonial responsibility. World Schools of
Colonialism morph into World Schools, Schools of the Americas, Schools of International Relations, Schools of Global
Studies...In that sense, King Leopold's spirit continues to ani-
mate the dominant West.

But there is a subaltern West and I see that subalternity flour-
ishing and perishing all around me. Its presence is calligraphed,
sometimes, on those bodies that have been inadequately educated in their colonial responsibilities. Jeffrey Lucey, 23, was
one such colonial—but not human—failure.[15] A Lance Corpo-
ral in the Marine Reserves who served six months in Iraq as a
truck driver, he was ordered to shoot two unarmed Iraqi soldiers. He did. But, try as he might, he could not come to terms
with his killings or the emotional agony that it brought him.
Neither the flag nor the therapist could get him to relocate
responsibility for his ordered murders onto some other body.
He insisted on defining himself as a murderer. He sought some
refuge from that honesty in a touching, child-like, humanity,
occasionally asking his father if he could sit in his lap. Finally,
unable to cope with the grievous burden that a brutal and
insensitive-to-its-own colonial state had privatized onto his
body, he hanged himself in his parents' home. The doctors now
present the many traces of his attempt to recover his humanity,
as manifest in his seeking of a refuge in his father's lap, as
"signs of regression, symptoms shown by suicidal people trying to cling to an emotionally safe memory."[16] If this is regression, don't we need more of it? I mourn the two unarmed Iraqi
soldiers that Jeffrey Lucey killed on orders. I also mourn
Lucey's subsequent killing of himself. To his credit, he could
not get himself to treat only the other as dispensable. Tragic as
it is, it is bodies such as these that hold the impossible and
incredible possibility of a provincialized West. The urgent pro-

ject might be to reach out to them before the colonial institutions reach them. It is in these preemptive efforts or more successful redemptive strategies that the promise of a more provincial and hence more humane West, one that would affirm and make Life rather than History, appears to be manifest.

I feel no glee as I await the development of this Other West.

VI

Combating Comfort

Suicides among soldiers in 2008 rose for the fourth year in a row, reaching the highest level in nearly three decades, Army officials said Thursday. At least 128 soldiers killed themselves last year, and the Army suicide rate surpassed that for civilians for the first time since the Vietnam War, according to Army statistics. The suicide count, which includes soldiers in the Army Reserve and the National Guard, is expected to grow. ...

"This is not business as usual," said Gen. Peter W. Chiarelli, the vice chief of staff of the Army, who is leading suicide-prevention efforts. "We need to move quickly to do everything we can to reverse the very disturbing number of suicides we have in the US Army."

The Army did not identify a specific reason for the increase, but officials said fifteen-month deployments to war zones played a role. These deployments, which have allowed for little time away from the battlefield, have contributed to post-traumatic stress disorder, depression, alcohol abuse and family problems. Seven suicides took place in Afghanistan and thirty-one in Iraq.[17]

GIBSON: One thing you'll miss most?

BUSH: Well, I'll miss being Commander-in-Chief. I have gotten to be—grown to be so appreciative of our military. It's hard to believe that so many kids, and some not-so-kids, have volunteered to fight in a war. And I'll miss—and it's going to sound strange to you—I'll miss meeting with the families whose son or daughter have fallen in combat, because the meetings I've had with the families are so inspirational. They—I mean, obviously, there's a lot of sadness, and we cry, and we hug, and we occasionally laugh. And we share—I listen to stories. But the Comforter-in-Chief is always the comforted person.[18]

2

NUMB AND NUMBER

I

History

Amidst the horror and pain of the war in Iraq, I must confess to a little bit of glee recently. It was not without some pleasure, on 14 December 2008, that I watched Muntadhar al-Zaidi's shoes sail towards President Bush. The video seemed to surge and scream as shoes and words hurtled themselves from the viewer's, normally seated, and numbingly passive, position. Unable to suffer any longer the indignity of a sneaky and blithe farewell—what does a goodbye mean after you have invited yourself in and wrecked my place—he stood up and hurled shoe after shoe laced with some choice, if also poignant, sentences. Not quite turning one's cheek, but a human(e) response nevertheless. Smarter, gentler and more precise, wouldn't you say, than those bombs and missiles with arrogantly scrawled messages perennially raining from the podium side?

Precision? Maybe you wish to quibble, gently and silently, with that choice. Al-Zaidi's precision lay not in his two shoes finding a face (which they didn't) but in their slapping us from our numbness, from a state in which we all know the horror but fail to feel anything. Straying across the secured zone from which speaker-bombers constantly drone over the spoken-bombed, Al-Zaidi dropped some presents of his own: First, a kiss, a bitter one without doubt, on behalf of a people shocked and sundered, though not shocked enough to stop them from talking back ("This is a gift from the Iraqis; this is the farewell kiss, you dog!"); and then, another, from the million dead and the millions more down-sliced by those murders ("This is from the widows, the orphans and those who were killed in Iraq!"). Seeing, as he put it later, "the flow of the blood of innocents" in Bush's "icy smile," Al-Zaidi's limbs, lips and shoes came together to smack us, if only for a few filmic moments, on our thinking-feeling about Iraq.

Well, how do we think-feel about that war?

Some numbers to begin with: So far, more than a million killed and millions more "displaced."[1] But if we dared not disturb the dead at present, then Professor Juan Cole gives us one description of what's happened to the other millions or in what ways they are out-of-place: "An estimated 4 million Iraqis, out of 27 million, have been displaced from their homes, that is, made homeless. Some 2.7 million are internally displaced inside Iraq. A couple of hundred thousand are cooling their heels in Jordan. And perhaps a million are quickly running out of money and often living in squalid conditions in Syria. Cheney's war has left about 15 per cent of Iraqis homeless inside the country or abroad. That would be like 45 million Americans thrown out of their homes."[2]

Forty-five million Americans thrown out of their homes. Now that's a number. If you brought that home another way, it would be somewhat like the forty-three million or so without health care, or out-of-place in terms of health care, in the US. But rather than focus on and translate this larger context of horror—"the flow of the blood of innocents"—that Al Zaidi was outraged about, many reporters decided to stick to the dog and shoes show. What ensued was the sorry spectacle of US reporters scrambling to explain to their readers the cultural significance of shoes and dogs rather than the crimes in question:[3]

> Hitting someone with a shoe is considered the supreme insult in Iraq. It means that the target is even lower than the shoe, which is always on the ground and dirty. Crowds hurled their shoes at the giant statue of Mr. Hussein that stood in Baghdad's Firdos Square before helping American marines pull it down on 9 April 2003, the day the capital fell. More recently in the same square, a far bigger crowd composed of Iraqis who had opposed the security agreement flung their shoes at an effigy of Mr. Bush before burning it.[4]

Given their rapid honing in and droning on and on about shoes and dogs as if they were the primary site of explanatory significance ("It's the shoe, stupid!"), one couldn't but wonder about the abundant avenues for scholarly analysis here: If "hitting someone with a shoe" is the "supreme insult" in Iraq, what does that action mean elsewhere in the world, say in Iran or Israel? Or, if those two countries cannot be compared properly with Iraq, what does being hit with a shoe (or being called a dog) signify in the US or Canada? Would that be less than a "supreme insult" or a commendation? And what of the defensive actions of ducking shoes when they are hurled at you? Was Nur al-Maliki's maneuver of extending a hand culturally different from Bush's ducking? Did it show a collective spirit as against Bush's individual regard? The possibilities for reading a "clash of cultures," for "signaling," for figuring out offensive and defensive cultural capabilities or for communicating credibility suddenly appeared very promising. Maybe this was a new growth area for comparative analysis.

Warming up to the comparative analysis of national-cultures, what exactly did it mean to "gift" shoes to a visiting head of state, a self-styled "comforter-in-chief"? Did it testify to the perennially "hospitable" nature of the natives, generous to a fault to the messiahs and the Gods who come to save them periodically? Or, did it signify their inability to overcome "traditional" patterns of exchange even at the level of offensive behavior? How is it that the Iraqi natives who presumably look down upon dogs as the lowest of the low still deign to kiss them when bidding farewell? Did that mean that a kiss was not just a kiss in the Iraqi mind-heart? Or, given that the typical Iraqi's feet and shoes are at one end while their lips are at another, that one is closest to the dirt while the other the furthest from it, given these two polarities, what does it mean for the Iraqi Al-Zaidi to mix shoes and kisses so provocatively? Was that a deliberate and devious effort to confuse us as we struggled to win their "hearts" or does it reveal to us the irrationalities and incoherencies of their (very Arab) "mind" and their unconscious desires to be assaulted and liberated simultaneously? One could dig into this so deeply and single-mindedly that the real outrage would never register on anyone, least of all, the self.

Moreover, this suddenly felt need to unravel the culturally specific meanings of shoes or the hierarchies of dogs and kisses (as well as kisses conveyed through shoes for dogs) within "Arab" or "Iraqi culture" differed significantly from the relative lack of enthusiasm or interest in explaining, some years earlier, the widely-touted expectations of flowers and garlands as welcoming presents for liberators. Were flowers then the universal symbols of love and liberation while shoes and dogs are only parochial expressions? Were the current demonstrations and expressions of support for Al-Zaidi across Iraq and the world a reflection of the surprising familiarity and spread of Arab customs across the world or just a case of your usual "anti-Americanism"? What do these Al-Zaidis of the Third World really want? What was he, Al-Zaidi, thinking?

Put on trial, Muntadhar al-Zaidi, pleaded not guilty, saying primarily that he was overcome by passion because of the suffering of the people of Iraq. "In that moment, I saw nothing but Bush, and I felt the blood of the innocents flowing under his feet while he was smiling that smile," he said at his hearing.[5]

That blinding insight earned him a three-year prison sentence from an Iraqi court for the crime of assaulting a visiting head of state.

It is reported that some members of his family responded to the verdict by saying: "It's an American court... sons of dogs."[6]

II

Monuments

One of the groups inspired more positively by Al-Zaidi's action were the children of an orphanage in Tikrit, Iraq. Seeking to translate the video memory of Al-Zaidi's action into something more enduring and grounded, they and a sculptor, Laith al-Amiri, "erected a brown replica of one of the shoes" thrown by Al-Zaidi. Made of fibreglass and coated with copper, the monument was reported to be 11.5 feet in height with the shoe portion of it being 8.2 feet in length and 4.9 feet in width. Estimated at having cost approximately $5,000, it was "built in fifteen days and opened to the public on Tuesday, 27 January 2009."[7] So much for the numbers that were reported but what did the children see in this monument?

According to the director of the orphanage, Faten Abdulqader al-Naseri, "Those orphans who helped the sculptor in building this monument were the victims of Bush's war," and this was their "gift to the next generation to remember the heroic action by the journalist." One act of gift-giving had thus set off another and would probably, it was hoped, spark some conversations about the crime of occupation.

"When the next generation sees the shoe monument, they will ask their parents about it," al-Naseri said. "Then their parents will start talking about the hero Muntadhir al-Zaidi, who threw his shoe at George W. Bush during his unannounced farewell visit." While Al-Zaidi's gift provoked a focus on shoes and dogs among US reporters, the children's gift was meant to spark conversations between Iraqi parents and children about journalistic heroes and heroic acts during a war of occupation. This was, presumably, a loving, not a bitter, kiss from orphaned victims to more fortunate children to never forget.

But, just as these orphans were etching their gift of memory to the next generation, in the hope of conversations to come, one of the people responsible, President Bush, was busy giving out exit interviews in order to shape future conversations about what occurred during his eight years in office.[8]

In one of these interviews reporter Martha Raddatz questioned President Bush about the shoes thrown at him on his farewell visit to Iraq. But her way of asking the question itself was intriguing: "Let's start with what just happened. And that is someone threw a shoe at you, whether it's an Iraqi reporter? (sic)"

Isn't there a certain strangeness to the questioning itself? (Or rather a familiarity?) By casting the shoe-thrower (well-known from the very beginning of the coverage) as the seemingly unknown ("someone") element, isn't Raddatz changing the force of the question, turning it to an issue of the thrower's professional identity ("whether it's an Iraqi reporter?") rather than drawing attention to its larger context and significance? Did she really need Bush to confirm the identity of the shoe-thrower or was she, by her way of posing the question, evacuating the larger significance of Al-Zaidi's action?

Bush responded by picking up (and therein lies the familiarity, the intimacy of knowing what was being offered to him) the cue ("Yeah, I think it's a reporter. At least that's what they told me on the way out, that it's a person who works in the Iraqi press, stands up and throws his shoe"), answering the question and then going on to represent its significance in terms of its utmost "weirdness" ("And it was amusing. I mean, I've seen a lot of weird things during my presidency and this may rank up there as one of the weirdest") while quickly connecting it to another event ("On the other hand, I do remember when the president of China came to the South Lawn, and a member of the press corps started yelling, I think it was Falun Gong slogans, at the Chinese president. So this happens and it's a sign of a free society") on the more familiar home terrain.

Raddatz and Bush thus perform a dance whose net effect is to turn our attention away from the dripping of "the blood of innocents" and towards the "weirdness" of those who might dare draw our attention to it, all the while appearing to celebrate the ideals of their "free society."

Do weird and amusing things happen in a free society? Really? In the space of a few sentences, the fearless reporter of a free society and the leader of the free world have managed to take an event motivated by the unwarranted deaths of a million people, and turned it into a testament to the strangeness of the messenger himself while touting the virtues of the killing society.

Living in a free society, Raddatz did not bother to question whether Bush knew or wondered about what had led Al-Zaidi to undertake such a risky venture (one report mentioned that he expected to be killed by the body guards surrounding Bush and Nur al-Maliki and so had already said his last prayers). But Al-Zaidi himself clearly did not realize how lucky he was to be occupied by a free society!

Living in a free society, Raddatz did not alert Bush to the fact that Al-Zaidi was brutally beaten ("They kicked him and beat him until 'he was crying like a woman,' said Mohammed Taher, a reporter for Afaq, a television station owned by the Dawa Party, which is led by Mr. Maliki")[9] as he was led out or the possibility that he was also tortured in custody even while being charged with the crime of "committing aggression against a foreign head of state," a charge that earned you at least seven years in prison in an Iraq freed through an unjust and unpopular aggression.

But leaving aside all that a Martha Raddatz could have done, living in a free society, to point out the less amusing and more deathly side of this event to Bush (presuming he was unaware of them), she tried, once more, to push the question further, highlighting the meaning of the event as it appeared to her: "It's also considered a huge insult in this world, the sole of a shoe, throwing a shoe."

In thus venturing forth, was she consulting him about whether this was an insult? Or, whether he thought this was an insult, since "in this world" (she really means "over there," doesn't she?), it was considered one? Or, was this maybe her own "heroic" moment, her way of asking: why was someone so bent on insulting you?

Continuing the dance, Bush took the cue again and proceeded to instruct her (and us) on what the event meant and who was insulted and how: "I guess. Look *they* were humiliated. The press corps, the rest of the Iraqi press corps was humiliated. These guys were just besides themselves about, they felt like he had disgraced their entire press corps and I frankly, I didn't view it as, I thought it was interesting, I thought it was unusual to have a guy throw his shoe at you. But I'm not insulted. I don't hold it against the government. I don't think the Iraqi press corps as a whole is terrible. And so, the guy wanted to get on TV and he did. I don't know what his beef is. But whatever it is I'm sure somebody will hear it."[10]

If you haven't understood the meaning of the event yet, this was the moment of clarity, of clear instruction. The insult was clearly their problem, not Bush's. It was an insult to them, to the Iraqis, the Iraqi press corps and the government. They were humiliated. He only thought it was "interesting" and "unusual." Was he insulted, maybe by a breach in the standards of protocol upheld by the Iraqi government or the Iraqi press corps? Of course not.

We thus have a situation in which one reporter sees a million dead in an "icy smile" and can no longer contain himself. Another, from a free society, who can't quite get what the fuss is and hesitates to press the smiling comforter-in-chief. Of course, unlike in an occupied society, where orphans can jump-start smart and significant conversations, in a free society, you are free not to converse, free not to understand; free not to ask why people are risking their lives and bodies to hurl things at you. Free to assume it might be to get on TV, free to find all the fuss a bit "weird" and "amusing." But, in a free society, would anyone care (or should I say, will anyone dare) to tell the leader of the free world that he was getting slapped because his smile was oozing the wrong colors?

Self-Monumentalization

Viewing the footage from another angle, *New York Times* columnist, Roger Cohen, in an op-ed piece titled "Two shoes for democracy," had a seemingly different analysis.[11] Reading Al-Zaidi's action, not in relation to Iraqi culture, but in the broader context of US policy under Bush and the division of Iraq into Green and Red Zones, Cohen analyzed their continued separation as a "monument to failure" and as a symptom of the "hollow" nature of Iraqi democracy because "It is openness, accessibility and accountability that distinguish democracies from dictatorships. Or it should be. A country governed from a fortress inaccessible to 99 per cent of its citizens may be many things, but is not yet a democracy." Situated thus, Cohen read Al-Zaidi's "gesture" as one that: "...broke those barriers, penetrated the hermetic sealing, and brought Red-Zone anger to Green-Zone placidity. In this sense, his was a democratic act." Cohen then elaborated its meanings:

> What it said was: "Tear down these walls." What it summoned was the deaths, exile and arbitrary arrests that US incompetence has inflicted on countless Iraqis—a toll on which al-Zaidi has reported. What it did was thrust Bush, for a moment, out of the comfort zone of his extravagant illusion. Perhaps, for a second, the other shoe dropped.

I find Cohen's reading of Al-Zaidi's act in the context of US occupation and as a democratic gesture really significant here, especially since it acknowledges the anger of those at the receiving end of the carnage accompanying the invasion. And it is not inconceivable that Al-Zaidi may have been demanding that those walls separating the Green from the Red Zone be torn down. Cohen's reading, unlike many of the others, places Al-Zaidi's actions more directly in their immediately political context rather than in a putatively cultural one that hones in, however precisely and rigorously, on questions of shoes and dogs.

But then, as Cohen goes on to expound on the theme of democracy, we see the problematic nature of the political context that he does take for granted: "After the incident, I heard from a US friend now serving in the joint security station in Sadr City, the teeming Shiite district of Baghdad from which al-Zaidi hailed. He wrote:

> We did not get a fusillade of shoes thrown over the concrete barriers and razor wire. One college engineering student in Sadr

basically said re: the press conference incident: "Well that's the democracy you brought us, right?" Or rather, it was a glimmering of such a democracy.

Why a glimmering, one could ask? That's the question that Cohen sets us up to ask but also goes on to answer in a particular way:

Anyone throwing a shoe at Saddam Hussein would have been executed, along with numerous other members of his family, plus assorted friends, within hours of such an incident. Iraq is slowly learning the give-and-take of a system where differences are accommodated rather than quashed. But the process is slow. Recovering from murderous despotism takes *a minimum of a generation*.[12]

Now this is where the limits of Cohen's reading, its fundamentally colonial nature, begin to appear. The engineering student, as conveyed to us through Cohen's conversation with his friend, ostensibly equates democracy with the right to dissent, as exemplified by the throwing of the shoe. Fair enough. But was such dissent, an act of defiance and protest, something that could have come only with or after the US invasion? Does Cohen expect us to believe that there was no defiance, no dissent, no "supreme insults" directed against authority figures (no authority figure denigrated as a dog) before the US invasion of Iraq in 2003? Was the present generation, the generation of Iraqis present, lacking in heroic and/or dissenting and democratic actions because they are presumed to have lived under a dictator? Does it take a generation of learning (of occupied teachings?) to overcome that lack? What sort of a present is Cohen offering us? What sort of gifts are such representations?

Cohen would probably not say that there was no such resistance but more that any such resistance would have been squashed brutally by Saddam Hussein. That is, a "murderous despot" would have "executed" the dissenters along with their family members "within hours." So people could dissent but their dissent would not have been "accommodated" within the [Iraqi] system. Whatever else the US might have done, however horrible the consequences of the invasion, whatever the bungling, it had still brought the "gift" of democracy, a glimmer of it at least, to the Iraqis, if only because you were not likely to be executed for dissenting acts such as throwing shoes.

Bush was incompetent (and Al-Zaidi can, and we also must, criticize him, Cohen seems to say) but Saddam was despotic and murderous (Al-Zaidi could not have criticized him and our words would not have mattered to Hussein; and what can't you think of one for whom words don't matter?). Bush bungles and lives in a delusional world from which he could be shaken but Saddam lived in a world in which he ruthlessly and competently killed all dissenters and their close friends and relatives ("within hours of such an incident"). The actions of both resulted in the deaths of many. But, really, would you want a bungling Bush or a murderously ruthless Saddam ruling over Mr. Al-Zaidi?

Saddam's presence, in Cohen's reading, overwhelms all of Iraq and its millions of Iraqis, making their dissent, their resistance, or the very thought of any heroic action on their part, impossible to conceive. While his actions may not have resulted in the million dead that Bush's have, they do carry the suffocating mark of the foreign, the strange, the weird (the despotic and murderous Other). That smothering Otherness marks the sign of Iraq so strongly that it makes it impossible to imagine dissent in the present. It has to await a later future, a later generation, maybe a generation later.

If Saddam's presence smothers the Iraqi real, then Bush's presence seems to leave the real underwhelmed (notwithstanding the million dead and the millions homeless) in Cohen's reading. Bush's mark here speaks primarily to the realm of incompetence, of illusion, of a comfort that needs to be disturbed. Reality grows against Bush's delusions, in spite of his comforts and beliefs and his extravagant assumptions. And dissent and democracy continue to thrive in that reality and force themselves against his delusions, maybe even penetrating them sometimes. So you can have contempt for Bush but his actions don't seem foreign or strange; they are only a poorer or exaggerated version of the self (of the incompetent or extravagant self) but not that of a threatening Other.

Is there then really a choice here? Hasn't Cohen also delivered to the Iraqis, even after vehemently criticizing Bush and the occupation, the structural present of American democracy, the gift of the self? Hasn't he presented the contrast in such a fashion that, notwithstanding all the qualifications, one cannot but say that the "glimmer of democracy" under Bush is (somehow) better than the despotism of a Saddam?

What Cohen gift-wraps for us then is a seeming comparison and choice between a US self that is, at its worst, incompetent and another, presumably Iraqi, self that, at its (past/previous) best, is "murderously despotic" if highly "competent" ("would have been executed, along with numerous other members of his family, plus assorted friends, *within hours* of such an incident"). The incompetence/competence, US/Iraqi binary, however, plays ironically on a deeper one of the human/inhumane binary between Bush and Saddam. Bush's incompetence is, paradoxically, also a sign of his humanness and the potentially humane. Humans make mistakes; do idiotic, incompetent and unthinking things. But they can also be insulted, hit with shoes, criticized, called names, made fun of; they can duck, apologize, be better or worse, be forgiven or change; in other words, to be human is to have the potential to go against one's previous actions and make history. To be human is to be recuperated, to have the potential to be recuperated, into the realm of the historical. Bush, for all his idiocy and incompetence, is still human for Cohen.

Murderous despots, on the other hand, are on the margins of humanity; they are dangerous and deadly because of their very nature, their very essence. There is only one outcome (of course, you can read them, you know their likely actions even when they are dead) if you insult them, throw shoes at them or dissent in any form from their murderous commands. The actions of both bungling democrats and butchering despots might result in mass deaths but only one of them functions in the arena of humanity and politics (of bungling, learning, living, accommodating, getting along) while the Other is in the realm of nature and necessarily outside politics and history. Your only engagement with the Other here will be in terms of containing or eliminating the possibility of murder, torture and other forms of violence that ensue from the essential nature of despotism. There is no space for a viable resistance or historically significant change here but only the possibility of submission to those dictates or that of violent resistance.

If Al-Zaidi is brave in his dissent, that bravery cannot but also be an implicit testimonial to the transformed essence, the reworked nature, of Iraqi society, a structural-historical change wrought by an invasion, however incompetent. Iraqis are slow in learning ("Iraq is slowly learning the give-and-take of a system where differences are accommodated rather than quashed. But the process is slow. Recovering from murderous despotism takes a minimum of a generation") but isn't that to be expected as they make the transition from a state of nature (and of essences) to the human condition, from being ruled (and killed arbitrarily) by murderous despots to being rescued (and injured and killed, un-arbitrarily?) by bungling presidents (at whom you can still throw shoes)?

The two cheers that Cohen gives to democracy end up as implicit cheers for the invading US self. Bush and Saddam are the foils that allow a self-congratulatory liberal-colonial imaginary to sneak, uninvited and unjustly like Bush, into the epistemic space of Iraq. We glaze over the innumerable lives shattered and the numbers of people screaming in pain due to the invasion as history; our recorded conversations are re-scripted to tell us that notwithstanding all the incompetence, something good, even if it's only a shimmering potential now, did come out of all the violence (which we condemn of course): that now, an ordinary journalist can throw shoes at the mighty and live (imagine that! How impossible before!).

We made that impossible possible for the ordinary Iraqi. We made and continue to make history. It's only the glimmers of democracy now (the natives are slow in recovering, learning or changing their essential character) but at least it's a start. However incompetently, whatever the violence, we still brought Iraq into the history of democracy. Imagine what we could do with better leadership. Imagine how much the rest of the world would benefit from our greater competence and our capacity to do the impossible for ordinary people everywhere. Only here. Only through our leadership:

> And so to all other peoples and governments who are watching today, from the grandest capitals to the small village where my father was born: know that America is a friend of each nation and every man, woman and child who seeks a future of peace and dignity, and that we are ready to lead once more.[13]

Which brings us, once again, to the issue of presents, of our presents to ourselves as well as the nature of the present.

III

Nature's Presence and Ours

Unlike the present, the dead were all over the TV in 2004. They kept floating up, flooding our screens in ways that were impossible to turn away from: 55,000, 60,000, 75,000 and, on the penultimate date of the year 2004, they stood at 115,000. It was not necessarily our business—it was happening oceans away—but you couldn't help hearing about them or seeing them plastered all over TV screens and magazine covers. A tsunami had wrought mass destruction in the Indian Ocean and, unlike the havoc of the Iraq war, the bloated and the brown were relentlessly tearing our eyes.

Overwhelmed by the numbers dead, I groped for the appropriate series, hoping that the form of the event and the grammar of causal analysis would somehow help me make sense of this mass destruction. Of course, the few years before that had been all about these insecurities and about not waiting till "smoking guns turned into mushroom clouds." Not surprisingly, the mushrooms over Hiroshima and Nagasaki and the number of bodies those forms might have contained flitted, briefly, across my mind; more than 200,000 maybe? So did the *Lancet* study of the hundreds and thousands of Iraqi deaths since the American invasion; also the 500,000 deaths of Iraqi children after the imposition of economic sanctions but before the "liberation."[14] International politics appeared not to be lacking in conceptual forms or causal analysis or even moral judgments that allowed one to try and make sense of death *en masse*.

There was a class of global events and a conceptual form for ordering them, such that one could contain and compare deaths that occurred in multiples of 100,000. But were there other ways, apart from in multiples of hundred thousands, to think, feel, connect and make sense of these deaths? Was there a way to improve the quality of our thinking about mass destruction: some more meaningful, qualitatively more humane way, perhaps?

This seemed important since number alone was not the crucial element here. Some of these deaths were the deliberate outcome of "history-making" events while others were attributable to "nature": some were ongoing but relatively invisible, while others couldn't be avoided visually; some were deemed a "price" that was "worth it" while others disappeared, were made absent, to mark the presence and power of science, technology and shock.[15]

Lego-like humans, dead but stackable, lent themselves creatively to multiple building blocks in international relations: "war," "liberation," "natural disaster," "economic sanctions," "super-power." Our concepts could contain, constrain or vaporize multitudes. But why did only some of them prey on our conscience while others needed to be dragooned into our minds? Why did some of them shock us while others drifted by, unwept and un-mourned?

Writing perceptively on the tsunami, Jonathan Schell (2005) pointed out an interesting reaction to the shock produced by the mass deaths: "[M]ost people around the world seemed disoriented by nature's shock. The human capacity for mass destruction has been so highly developed in our time that we seem, without quite realizing it, almost to have claimed title to the art, as if to say, "Wait, how can nature do this? Isn't killing hundreds of thousands of people *our* business?"

Is killing hundreds of thousands our business? Is that what shocks us about the tsunami while leaving us unmoved about Iraq? Is that what forces those dead bodies on our eyes, Nature's impudent claiming, its usurping, of a power that we see as ours alone? Is it our resentment at that transgression that makes all those brown and bloated worth mourning or at least paying attention to?

Mass Death in IR

Talk about mass destruction, in international relations, emerges from an impressive archive. The capacity to destroy *en*

43

masse is regarded, generally, as a sign of power—super-power. It is therefore a part of the study of strategy in international relations—grand strategy, nuclear strategy.

In analyzing "the strategy of Hiroshima," a classic text on nuclear strategy points out:

> To get the full benefit of the Manhattan project it was necessary to emphasize the unique and awesome properties of the bomb. After it had been noted in the Interim Committee that the effect of one bomb would not be that different from "any Air Corps strike of current dimensions," Oppenheimer pointed out that the "*visual effect* of an atomic bombing would be tremendous. It would be accompanied by a brilliant luminescence which would rise to a height of 10,000 to 20,000 feet." It was on the basis of this *spectacular* quality that those considering the use of the bomb began to move away from the previous, implicit, strategy of cumulative pressure to one of *maximum shock*.[16]

Two points are noteworthy about this passage.

First, mass destruction, as thought, talked and practiced in international relations, is as much about its effects on those watching, listening, feeling, as it is about the relatively more mundane aspect of killing hundreds of thousands of people. That is, the "visual effect," "spectacular quality," and "maximum shock" that is being strategized here is not just about those being killed (because they'd disappear quickly anyway) but also about the effects on those watching or being forced to watch, hear, feel and learn from the present and subsequently from the archive.

It is therefore not just a question of impressive numbers but also of impressing a sort of numbness on the Other, of inducing an aesthetic response, of wringing a very particular sort of response from its body. Hiroshima is not just the production of mass death but also an aesthetic performance that stuns one constituency through the targeted and spectacular killing of another. In this performance, accompanying the desire and capacity to kill one is also the desire to *impress* another audience with that killing.

Mass destruction involves, therefore, the strategy of producing a meaningful and interpretable relationship between those who destroy, those who are destroyed and those who are in a position to observe both. The strategy of mass destruction achieves its fullest meaning ("full benefit") when those who are watching/spectating are appropriately impressed (moved by the spectacle, shocked or stunned to a maximum degree) by the capacity and willingness of one set of humans to destroy others in the hundreds of thousands.

Second, what differentiates our capacity to destroy *en masse* from that of Nature's is the latter's relative lack of interest in "impressing" any one, any specific audience. The "visual effect" that Robert Oppenheimer is praising is not on those likely to be vaporized. They are the targets and objects of the bomb but not the primary spectators Oppenheimer has in mind (they could have been spectators too if the atomic bomb had been dropped on an uninhabited island, but that was ruled out as we will see below). Arguably, this is what makes mass destruction *our* business rather than Nature's. Nature can, like us, destroy on a mass scale but is, I would probably say, not interested in impressing us humans whereas for us the capacity to destroy *en masse* achieves its "fullest meaning" only when it is accompanied, simultaneously, by a suitably stunned, impressed and shocked audience.

I say only, only because the desire to impress the assumed audience appears to trump any "humanitarian" considerations that might have otherwise prevailed.

Witness for example the place of humans and humane considerations in the "strategy of Hiroshima":

Many nuclear scientists argued that to demonstrate the bomb's power would suffice, for the knowledge of its existence would be shock enough. The humanitarian advantages of this course were discounted because of *practical disadvantages*: failure, after a portentous announcement, could be counterproductive while the *full meaning* of success could be lost if a spectacular display was unaccompanied by equally spectacular destruction. The problem was to *induce a sense of hopelessness* in a people, still resisting despite immense suffering, by *impressing upon them* their *vulnerability* to an *unprecedented form of horror*.[17]

Humanitarian considerations appear secondary here to "practical disadvantages" which could possibly come in the way of our realizing the "full meaning of success." The audience here not only needed to know about the existence of this powerful new capacity to destroy, but also to understand its "full meaning" which meant that they needed to be moved to feel particular emotions ("hopelessness" and "vulnerability" to "horror") in connection with this new knowledge. What that required was not the attention of a specific audience itself but also a set of human beings available for that mass destruction. The "full meaning of success" meant then the spectacular and impressive staging of a mass sacrifice, a mass evaporation, of human beings.

Put differently, mass destruction, as a *meaningful* strategy, presumes working on multiple subjects (audiences, targets, actors), at multiple levels (aesthetic, psychological, physiological) with multiple intended effects (the production of truth and proof, the demonstration of power):

To throw the enemy off balance was precisely what was required [Henry] Stimson wrote in 1947: "I felt that to extract a genuine surrender from the Emperor and his military advisers they must be administered a *tremendous shock* which would carry convincing proof of our power to destroy the Empire." The atomic bomb was "more than a weapon of terrible destruction; it was *a psychological weapon*." He noted that Marshall was "emphatic in his insistence on the shock value of the new weapon."[18]

The strategy of mass destruction is a meaningful one and is seen as working not just by physical destruction but also by the production of multiple intended effects. An element of surprise was needed to dislocate the Other and make it discontinuous with itself in order to better produce a vulnerability to powerlessness and subsequent surrender:

> A key feature of a strategy of shock was that it required an element of *surprise*. Here there was a contrast with a strategy of cumulative pressure. If the aim was to convince the enemy of the horror ahead if resistance continued, then a declaration of intent to devastate the enemy's homeland was a natural part of the strategy. But, if the aim was to shock, surprise was necessary. General Marshall explained: "It's no good warning them. If you warn them there's no surprise. And the only way to produce shock is surprise."[19]

Jonathan Schell is therefore correct in noting our sense of surprise at the tsunami. We are surprised because we expect to be the ones to be causing mass deaths through surprise, not others, not even Nature. We make history. We undertake mass sacrifices.

But Schell is less on target with his reading of Nature's capacity to usurp our capability. This is because mass destruction involves not just the capacity to produce physical death but also an orchestration of its social meanings. The production of mass destruction then, as also our strategic study of it ("the art of distributing and applying military means to fulfill (sic) ends of policy"), has an irreducibly interpretive (and qualitative) dimension, i.e. it also involves the production, sustenance and enforcement of specific meanings or interpretations of the practices of mass destruction.

In other words, it is not enough, as in Nature, to produce mass destruction as in a massive amount of death. It is equally, if not more, important to produce the appropriate interpretations of that mass destruction (i.e. as "spectacle," "horror," "tremendous shock."). What that means is that the inter-subjective dimension, the social and interpretive relationship that ties the bombers to the bombed, the mass destroyers to those destroyed *en masse*, the "inter" part of international relations, is crucially alive and fundamentally at stake here. The quantity of dead and the quality/qualitative meanings of those deaths are both at stake.

Nature can produce the former but it cannot usurp the latter. Mass destruction is our business to the extent that destruction in international relations, destruction as strategy ("functional and purposive violence"), destruction as a set of discursive practices, relies on interpretive acts as crucial and constitutive aspects accompanying the physical capacity to annihilate human beings in the hundreds of thousands. What, then, is the nature of the "inter" in the international relations of mass destruction? How should we think of the politics of that inter-relationship as it mediates our relations of dislocation, discontinuity and destruction?

IV

The Politics of the Inter: Asserting Discontinuity

Acknowledging the mass deaths produced by the tsunami, the Bush administration described them initially as "involving loss and grief beyond comprehension"[20] but also, as a "wonderful opportunity"[21] for the US, and for others, especially those in the "Muslim world," to see "American generosity, American values in action."[22] In the face of mass death, we were being told that in terms of "loss and grief," this was an event that was beyond our comprehension. Notwithstanding that incomprehension, we were also being told that the event was available as an opportunity for exhibiting something positive, something virtuous about the American self. What relationship of the inter, of the Self and the Other, connects these two moves? Should incomprehension of the other never impede self-presentation, never come in the way of an opportunistic and self-aggrandizing display?

Claiming that a specific situation is one "involving loss and grief beyond comprehension" can, one must acknowledge, be read in a relatively positive light. It can be seen as indicating humility in the face of unspeakable tragedy. It might be read as an understanding of the insignificance of anything the self might utter in the face of massive suffering, a gesture towards the inadequacy of words to capture the world of loss, pain and grief.

However, that reading would leave some other questions unaddressed. When such statements come from policy-makers who have rarely, if ever, admitted to "incomprehension" in other cases, especially those involving issues of mass destruction and the loss and grief flowing from them, could one really read them as gestures of humility only? Coming from them, might these words not also have a prescriptive ring? Should we not be watching out for a pre-emptive political strike here?

Yes, one can and must read a singularity in the pain and suffering inflicted on thousands of human beings by the tsunami—a singularity that, I recognize, cannot ever be fully "comprehended."

The picture of a mother, sprawled on the sand, mourning her child at the edge of the now calm and seemingly indifferent ocean springs powerfully to mind. An expression in Telugu—for me a language of familial intimacy—arrives unsummoned as I see that photograph: *kadupu kotha*. Those words connote the raw pain—the chopped up sensations—of the sundered-womb that lines your child's death. I turn to a friend better versed in Telugu literature for confirmation but he deflects my request for clarification claiming his own singularity: this might be too cinematic and not scholarly enough for his talents. Possibly. I cannot say that I have partitioned those aspects—the scholarly and the cinematic—of my life neatly enough but whether it is scholarly or filmic, I wish to be open to it as those words usher home a stranger's pain through a familial path.

Wondering about that commonality, one that arrives uninvited (but is not unwelcome) in the face of the Other's tragedy and pain, one can ask: isn't there, in the suffering of other humans, something that one can relate to as a parent, sibling, son, fellow human, or a student of politics? If it was the scale of destruction and the corresponding "loss and grief" that the US President was focused on, then wasn't destruction at that level at least gesturing, even if only in an indirect and messy way possibly, to the mass destruction, the hundreds of thousands of dead, in Iraq? Why was it then that this event was being defined as one "beyond our [and not just his], comprehension"? What exactly was beyond comprehension here?

An administration that had generated endless fear and insecurity about "mass destruction," painted apocalyptic scenarios of "mushroom clouds," never let its lack of comprehension of many international issues hold back its unilaterally aggressive moves, what did it mean for that administration to suddenly claim that certain events of mass destruction were beyond everyone's comprehension, theirs but ours too? With what authority could the US President mark a global event as so singular that it is outside of "our," not solely his, comprehension? Was this a position of epistemic humility or colonial arrogance? What politics, politics of the mass destruction of meaning, I began to wonder, motivated this move?

The attempt to place this event as one "beyond our comprehension" is, I will argue below, a specifically colonial enunciation of the discourse on mass destruction. It is part of an attempt that seeks to sequester and thus secure the dominant understanding of events by defining either their singularity or their universality at different times and various spaces. In doing this it seeks to shape the inter- of international relations and it is this constitution of the inter in a specifically unilateral way that produces mass destruction as a problem of the Other in international politics. Given such conditions of enunciation, the concept of mass destruction must be rescued from its constant production within a colonial discourse. In order to do that, it is important to reconfigure somewhat the existing insights of postcolonial theory as they apply to international politics.

V

The Colonial Imaginary

In a classic article titled "Number in the Colonial Imagination," Arjun Appadurai traced a variety of ways in which enumeration played a crucial role in the administrative logic and politics of the modern colonial state.[23] Asking "what special role does the enumeration of bodies have under colonial rule?" he suggested that "numbers were a changing part of the colonial imaginary and function[ed] in justificatory and pedagogical ways as well as in more narrowly referential ones."[24] While Appadurai was talking about the nature of the colonial state historically, there is much that is relevant in his theorizing to an analysis of contemporary international relations.

The "numerical gaze" has functioned quite well in a number of ways in the contemporary international system. It has, among other things, acted to constitute, unilaterally, the ostensibly universal and seemingly objective character of the categories and modes of knowing of the colonizer.

Tintin in the Congo

The comic strip *Tintin* offers a particularly good example of this universalizing function. Published in Belgium, and popular in much of the world (though less so in the US), one of the earliest strips deals with Tintin's adventures in Africa ("Tintin in the Congo"). In this particular strip, Tintin goes to visit a mission in the Congo and, as he is led around by the "good Father" from the mission station, expresses his admiration for the hospital and the farm school (Tintin: "It's marvellous!" His dog: "What a nice place!" "Missionaries are the tops!"). Pointing to a chapel, the Father notes, "When we first arrived here a year ago, this place was bush." When the "good Father" has to substitute for a teacher who's fallen sick, Tintin volunteers, in his place, to "give the lesson" in geography.

Tintin is then shown standing in front of Congolese children, pointing to a map of Belgium and telling them, "My dear friends, today I'm going to talk to you about your country: Belgium!" Even as he is instructing the natives, the classroom space is interrupted by a leopard that walks casually into it. Unfazed Tintin deals smoothly with the leopard as well as the Congolese children.[25]

This particular issue, first published in 1930, apparently encountered questions of "colonial attitudes." As the foreword to a 2002 unrevised edition (emphasis added) points out, "In his portrayal of the Belgian Congo, the young Hergé reflects *the colonial attitudes of the time*. He himself admitted that he depicted his Africans according to *the bourgeois, paternalistic stereotypes of the period*." It adds, no doubt helpfully, "The same may be said of his treatment of big-game hunting and his attitude towards animals." Clearly, the problem lay with the "colonial attitudes" and "paternalistic stereotypes" of the time.[26]

Much could be said of the ways in which the assertion of being with the times is offered as an explanation for and exculpation of a colonial perspective. That was then. This is now. The "that was then" argument comes across not as an apology but as a matter-of-fact claim/demand to understand and situate the (colonizing) self: It is a surprise to see such attitudes towards the Africans and animals but that's just how things were then! Nowadays, we are civilized enough to see both animals and natives as deserving better treatment or better representation at least.

Such a move is particularly interesting since part of the colonial strategy is "the denial of co-evalness" to the Other, the always-already "not yet" nature of the colonized.[27] The colonizers' problem, it appears, is that when they are not with the times, they are insufficiently ahead of them (inadequately avant-garde). The colonized, on the other hand, are never really ready for, or with, the times. Not even in their stereotypes. Time functions to hobble the colonized but always marches in step with the colonizers, or is behind them. One is dislocated/shocked/displaced by time while the other is always located, in place and possibly at home. One is made, re-made, and made over by history while the other makes it (or if not, is at least in tune with it).

But it is not the account in the foreword that is interesting as much as the nature of the scenes in the revised editions. In the revised depictions of these scenes, Tintin is still led around the mission and shown the hospital and the farm school and the chapel by the Father who makes the same comment about how before they came here, this place was bush. The difference this time is that Tintin remains silent in the frame. He is no longer shown saying, "It's marvellous!" And the dog is relatively taciturn too, no longer saying that the mission is a "nice place." But it does stick to its other original comment: "Missionaries are the tops!" In addition to this, the map disappears as a mode of instruction. We now see Tintin standing before a board with numerals ("2+2") and saying to his class: "We will start with some additions. Who can tell me how much two plus two equals? Nobody? ... Let us see, two plus two?"[28]

There are many interesting issues here in terms of the revisions seen as appropriate or necessary for new times. What the reconfiguration does, as is clear, is to separate Tintin from any direct approval of the missionizing aspect of colonial domination. So Tintin is now silent about his views on the mission, the farm-school, the hospital and the chapel. That job is delegated to his dog though with some minor changes. The place may or may not be nice but the missionaries are still "the tops." The "good Father" still gets to present the transformation of the landscape as presenting a no doubt positive movement from nature to civilization i.e. from "undeveloped bush" to sacred Chapel and the humanitarian institutions of a hospital and a school. Tintin's role is now focused directly on the schoolroom where his temporary burden involves the instruction of Congolese children not on problematic maps but on mathematical (presumably objective) logic.

A colonial discourse thus apologizes for not being sufficiently ahead of the times (we were not behind, only in tune with it; sorry!), and then reconfigures itself to the terrain of seemingly incontestable reason/logic while leaving the apparently more contestable aspects of its mission to its sidekicks ("running dogs of colonialism?") and other minor characters. The hero remains silent and speaks reason. The humanitarians speak of development and the poodles praise the humanitarians.

Maps are reconfigured into numbers and the now transparently, embarrassingly, subjective realm of geographical home is transformed into the seemingly objective realm of mathematical logic.

I expect that the revisions partly entailed the premise that unlike politically problematic geography (is Belgium the home country of the Congolese or the country that occupies their home?), numbers would be seen as objective and universal and thus seemingly without the taint of politics and particularity, representing, in that sense, the "cleanest" form of modern reason. After all, how could anyone object to Tintin teaching mathematics to a group of Congolese children? Don't you expect him to be at home there?

I have gone into some detail here to emphasize that the "numerical gaze" remains a crucial component of a colonial discourse even as it adapts itself to contemporary criticisms. But that numerical gaze now functions with a reconfigured strategy for relating to the Other. What is relevant, for us, is this changing configuration as it appears in a number of additional instances.

The US in Iraq

Asked about the number of Iraqi casualties in the US-led "liberation" of that country, General Tommy Franks replied, "We don't do body counts." This response can be seen as dictated, in many ways, by the much criticized, earlier history of implementing "production quotas" and generating "body counts" in Vietnam.[29] Given the discrediting of that earlier strategy, was a count of the Other now irrelevant or unnecessary? There is some reason to believe that General Franks' response was the preferred "public" face of the US military rather than any dramatic internal change in war strategy. This was indicated to some degree by a secret memo leaked in 2003 in which Donald Rumsfeld, the US Secretary of Defense, commenting on the "lack [of] metrics" needed to know whether the US was "winning or losing the global war on terror," wondered if the US was "capturing, killing, or deterring and dissuading more terrorists every day than the madrassas and the radical clerics are recruiting, training, and deploying against us."[30]

But, even if it remained relevant inside the administration, the numerical gaze was no longer the primary way of communicating one's mission, its successes and failures, to the public. A different sort of a missionary narrative had come to dominate it.

Witness, for instance, the response of an Operations Officer for the US Marines in Fallujah. On being asked about civilian casualties in Fallujah, Colonel Michael Regner replied, "...I just don't cover enemy killed in action. It's not a true reflection of the success that we've had in this battle to regain Fallujah for the good people of Iraq."[31] Number was now being projected as an unreliable indicator—"not a true reflection"—of events. What was important was that these actions needed to be read in the context of the goals being pursued for someone else, "for the good people of Iraq." But, like the presumed illiteracy/innumeracy of the Congolese children, the goodness of the people of Iraq was an article of faith that never required consulting them in the first place. Thus, if US military officers "conceived of themselves as business managers rather than combat leaders" in the "perfect," "technowar" in Vietnam,[32] the current phase of colonial governance seems to call upon them to play the role of "moral entrepreneurs" and "missionaries of liberty" in "pure" and "good" wars.

Word and narrative in the forefront, well ahead of the times; number and metrics behind.

That the "good fathers," the missionaries of liberty, could, on occasion, get carried away by their mission was evident in the statement of the deputy undersecretary of Defense for Intelligence Lt. General William G. "Jerry" Boykin who claimed that he knew he would prevail in the fight in Somalia since he knew that "his God was bigger than his [the Muslim "warlord's" in Somalia]. I knew that my God was a real God and his was an idol."[33]

Taking an even more enthusiastic posture towards his duties, Lt. Gen. James Mattis informed a San Diego Forum held by the Armed Forces Communications and Electronics Association and the US Naval Institute that:

Actually, it's a lot of fun to fight, you know. It's a hell of a hoot. It's fun to shoot some people. I'll be right upfront with you, I like brawling. You go into Afghanistan, you've got guys who slapped women around for five years because they didn't wear a veil. You know, guys like that ain't got no manhood left anyway. So it's a hell of a lot of fun to shoot them.[34]

Afghanistan is a place, a fun place, for those who "like brawling," and find fun in "shooting some sort of people," people-men without "manhood" who slap women around "because they didn't wear a veil." Afghanistan is where men with manhood (real men?) go to "shoot," to "shoot them," i.e. shoot men without manhood: Men without manhood who are neither men, nor women (who are slapped around) but—. Afghanistan is a hell of a place, it's "a hell of a hoot."

What is it that is seen as "controversial" about such statements? It is clear that these statements are problematic not necessarily because of what they reveal in terms of beliefs—neither of the Generals was fired—but because of indiscretion of saying such things when we are aware of the Other's presence as a listener, as a part of the international. As Stephen P. Cohen, a member of a special panel to study policy in the Arab and Muslim World for the US Advisory Commission on Public Diplomacy, noted: "The first lesson is to recognize that whatever we say here is heard there, particularly anything perceived to be hostile to their basic religion, and they don't forget it."[35]

The positive feature here is the acknowledgement of the Other's presence; the recognition that Others are listening and must be taken into account in one's public presentations. Like the publishers of Tintin, attention was now being paid to what the Other might say to one's depictions. But what is the nature of the adaptation here in the context of the Other that listens from there?[36] Are the here and the there being bridged by a mode of enunciation, an inter-national relationship, that is responsibly oriented toward each other or is it a discourse of coloniality reconfigured in new ways?

VI

Mass Destruction: Narratives of Origin

Viewed from the margins, the discourse of mass destruction reveals a basic asymmetry in its understandings of the international system. Though, analytically, this is a jointly constituted relationship, those who produce death *en masse* are distinctly different from the others who are forced to consume it collectively. Historically, one of the basic aspects of the discourse of mass destruction is a systemic asymmetry in the production, distribution and consumption of mass deaths. Even a cursory account of recent global history shows this uneven and asymmetric relationship—a relation in which the colonized have been destroyed *en masse* more times and in greater magnitude than any colonizer.[37] It is not just the asymmetry in deaths that I find troubling, or the almost uninterrupted continuation into the present of such a pattern. What is more disturbing is that this fundamental inequality seems not only to disappear, but to also reconfigure itself and re-emerge as a problem of the Other. The dominant idea of mass destruction, in much of conventional international relations theory and practice, is constructed and circulated predominantly as a threat from the Other to the Self.

Let me illustrate this point.

Stigmatizing the Other

The United States happens, historically, to be the first and only state so far to have rationally considered and used nuclear weapons deliberately. Not once, but twice.[38] Though the circumstances under which nuclear weapons might be deployed are subject to much debate, and there is obviously room for differences of opinion, the dominant international relations framework through which nuclear weapons (and other weapons of mass destruction) are analyzed appears impervious to both questions of rationality and loss of human life. On the contrary, the issue is constantly discussed in ways that reproduce the virtue of the US self and a fear of the rogue or proliferating Other. Thus, even in a time dominated by discussions of weapons of mass destruction, scholarly accounts of nuclear use in the international system revolve around discussions of a presumed nuclear taboo (e.g., Tannenwald, *The Nuclear Taboo*, 2007), nuclear proliferation (by rogue Others), or nuclear terrorism (Allison, "Lessons of Nagasaki for Fighting Terrorism," 2004).

The category of "nuclear taboo" acquires its meaningfulness by the conceptual (and exculpatory) qualification that these weapons have not been used by anyone since 1945. The fact that they were deliberately used twice by one state is seemingly not a problem for thinking about this issue. Nor is the fact that countries have been subsequently threatened and actually bombed with an explosive power that puts Hiroshima and

Nagasaki to shame. As James William Gibson, in pointing out the use of "bombing as communication" by the United States, notes:

> During World War II the United States dropped over two million tons of bombs and other munitions from aircraft. From 1965 through 1973, the United States dropped *at minimum* over eight million tons of munitions from aircraft onto Southeast Asia. The air war over Southeast Asia was thus the largest air war in world history. The United States did not use atomic weapons, but eight million tons is the equivalent in explosive force to 640 atomic bombs of the size used at Hiroshima. Paradoxically, the air war over North Vietnam is conventionally regarded as the most "limited" phase of a limited war.[39]

Against Gibson's comment, one must ask: is there really a paradox here or is this an essential part of the colonial translations of international events that IR produces?

Graham Allison, writing about the "lessons of Nagasaki for fighting terrorism," notes: "It produced an explosion greater than all the conventional bombs dropped by Allied forces on both Germany and Japan in the war."[40] He points out that while 70,000 people were killed in Nagasaki within four months, nearly half of the population of Nagasaki was dead in less than five years. And what is the lesson he intends to draw from this? That there is a "new nuclear threat in the form of terrorism" posed by Al-Qaeda. Though he recognizes that Al-Qaeda has a specific list of "strategic objectives," he also raises the prospect of an "unthinkable scenario." What is this scenario, a scenario "unthinkable" in ways that Hiroshima, Nagasaki and the bombings in Southeast Asia were so clearly not? "Unthinkable," apparently, is a situation in which "an American President would have to consider compromise."

Here, the substance of the compromise appears not to be the problem so much as the mere fact of having to compromise. The dangers of this scenario—the threat of compromise—do not lead Allison to explore the possibilities of a resolution that is truly global: universal nuclear disarmament. They do not lead him to consider the political objectives of those who might wish to bring about this "unthinkable scenario." He does not ask: why not see whether the "strategic objectives" of Al-Qaeda can be answered in other ways? What he wants to ensure primarily is that "no American president is ever left with no better choice than Emperor Hirohito." What is that choice? One reading of that could be that this choice is one of being "forced to surrender...to a terrorist's blackmail." This would have been an intriguing and potentially productive reading since it would have raised the issue of whether that was what the second American bomb was—blackmail—or at least to a consideration of it as a political choice that was not necessarily or easily justifiable. But that potentially critical reading is quickly foreclosed by Allison's insertion, in the ellipsis, of a few crucial and self-flattering assumptions: "forced to surrender, not to an army of liberation, but to a terrorist's blackmail."[41] The gap between the here and the there, the Self and the Other is bridged by the appropriation of seemingly unproblematic virtues for the Self. Compromise is unthinkable and can only be read as blackmail except when that blackmail is engaged in by the Self. Then that blackmail is understood to be "liberation." And the threat of this seemingly unthinkable scenario will not lead the Self to consider any resolution where both here and there, the Self and the Other, could be better off through a political engagement.

Purifying the Self

Nowhere is this strategy of the self constantly asserting and reclaiming its assumed virtues clearer than in discussions of humanitarian efforts on the part of the West in its colonial his-

61

tory. Adam Hochschild appears to have perfected this genre of research.[42] His works, commendably, draw attention to the atrocities inflicted on the colonized by various European powers. His narrative resolutions, however, after detailing the horrors of colonization, also, quite quickly, invoke a universality in which heroic European men and women resist, fight for the Others, and prevail to script global History. The Others, like the Congolese children, are silent, passive, or await instruction. In his recent book describing the efforts of the British Abolitionists to end slavery in the British Empire, Hochschild notes how the goal of the Abolitionists was "finally reached in 1838, a full quarter of a century before slavery died in the United States."[43] Fair enough, perhaps. There is a way to interpret that as a productive comparison. Abolitionists in Britain. Slavery in the United States. Something that the Self could learn from by comparison. But Hochschild moves quickly to secure the "universal" on behalf of a different Britain and a different US. He says:

> No more chained slaves cross the Atlantic today but the spirit that crystallized at George Yard is with us in a different way. In the idea that those who suffer "no grievance or injury" have the obligation to speak up for those who have suffered them lies the birth of the vision that human rights are universal.[44]

The slave-holding West has now been split into its good and bad parts. The good part not only does not suffer (and presumably does not benefit from the labor of the slaves in its territory), but lays claim to universality and avant-garde-ness in its access to the correct spirit—the "spirit that crystallized at George Yard."

What is this so-called spirit? Arising from a small anti-slavery movement that originated in a building that once stood at 2 George Yard in 1787, it refers to what Hochschild sees as a historically "unprecedented" movement: "It was the first time that a large number of people in one country became out-raged—and stayed outraged for many years—over the plight of other people, of another color, in other parts of the world."[45] Hochschild seems to me to be saying: while some of us here colonized or enslaved many of you over there or from there, others of us here, for the first time (here comes number, inno-vativeness and avant-garde-ness, being with or ahead of the times, again), were also outraged over you and your condition here and there. Time for Tintin's dog: "Missionaries are tops!" Hochschild thus bridges the gap between the here and the there, between the Self and the Other, by extending the borders of the virtuous self. Slavery, it appears once again, involves, "loss and grief beyond comprehension." But it is also a "won-derful opportunity" to showcase our values to those there. Even though some of us engaged in horrible deeds, others of us were brave and courageous enough to resist and combat them and win your release from their grasp. Let us take this oppor-tunity to hear the story of these wonderful beings and celebrate the values that allowed them to fight and pioneer in fighting on behalf of those to whom they had hardly any connection (i.e. you, you who are so dissimilar to us).

Here, here. It's all here. Bush, Rice, Powell, Obama. Tintin, his dog and the good Father. Hochschild and his universal (and necessarily Western) heroes. The Universe resides here, is recu-perated and resurrected here constantly. There is nothing there.[46] Only here.

> To those who cling to power through corruption and deceit and the silencing of dissent, know that you are on the wrong side of history, but that we will extend a hand if you are willing to unclench your fist.[47]

VII

Postcolonial Translations

In his preface to Frantz Fanon's *The Wretched of the Earth*, in 1961, Jean-Paul Sartre began by noting: "Not so very long ago, the earth numbered 2,000 million inhabitants, that is 500 million human beings and 1,500 million natives. The former possessed the Word, the rest borrowed it."[48] That "Golden Age," as Sartre notes, ended before 1961 itself. Today the earth numbers more than 6,000 million humans. Maybe a few million cannot but see others as natives. But a few hundred million, a billion here, another billion there, the global majority, possess both Word and Number. And Narrative and Metrics. They are there. And here too. They hear. And listen. And speak. And laugh. It is a Golden Age, of sorts. And the process of decolonization, thinking historically (being on the right side?), is just beginning.

What does it take, in this reconfigured global context, for colonial forms of governing the here and the there to re-assert themselves? What possibilities exist for postcolonial challenges to such resurrections? Drawing on a re-reading of postcolonial scholarship, I wish to argue that numbers present, notwithstanding their implications in colonial processes of administration, the possibility of a potentially alternative and possibly better way of bridging the here and there.

In highlighting the ways in which number served the colonial imaginary, Arjun Appadurai demonstrated that the critical role that number played came about:

> partly because it provided a shared language for information transfer, disputation, and linguistic commensuration between center and periphery, and for debates among a huge army of mediating bureaucrats...Number was thus part of the enterprise of *translating* the colonial experience into terms graspable in the

metropolis, terms that could encompass the ethnological peculi-
arities that various orientalist discourses provided.[49]

However, in a world governed by multiple loci of enunciation, numbers can be seen to possess various democratic and
progressive possibilities. That is, precisely because it is part of
"the enterprise of translating the colonial experience into terms
graspable in the metropolis," number, in providing a "shared
language," can allow social actors in various global centers to
relate imaginatively, with those in the peripheries in ways that
move beyond regressive, orientalist/colonial vocabularies. The
mass destruction caused by the 2004 tsunami was one good
example of a bridging of the here and there. The scale of suffering and destruction could be related to at many levels. But,
implicit in that relation, is also the capacity to then apply that
concept of destruction to make relative sense of other destruc-
tions. So much suffering in the region of the Indian Ocean. So
many children dead. Is that how it is in Iraq too? The terms of
understanding then can be fruitfully extended to render visible
and comprehensible that which otherwise was being rendered
invisible and incomprehensible. The fact that one was the primary effect of a "natural" process while the other was the
result of a more directly human enterprise only renders the ethical implications more starkly.

I cannot help thinking that it is this possibility of an ethically charged comparison, a knowledge of international relations that bridges the relationship between the here and the
there in a responsible and responsive way, that is sought to be
ruled out by the dominant discourse's naming of the "loss and
grief" generated as somehow unique, singular and "beyond
comprehension."

Whether this possibility of number offering a minimally
shared language for global solidarity will re-articulate or rein-
force colonial possibilities would hinge, quite obviously, on

various modes of translation across multiple loci of enuncia-tion. How should/could that translation take place? Elaborat-ing on this issue, Dipesh Chakrabarty notes:

> There remains something of a "scandal"—of the shocking—in every translation, and it is only through a relationship of inti-macy to both languages that we are aware of the degree of this scandal...It is all the more imperative, therefore, that we read our secular universals in such a way as to keep them open to their own finitude, so that the scandalous aspects of our unavoidable translations, instead of being made inaudible, actually reverber-ate through what we write in subaltern studies.[50]

"Keeping our secular universals open to their own finitude," in order to see that "the scandalous aspects of our unavoida-ble translations reverberate" between centers and peripheries then becomes an important issue for the generation of anti-colonial solidarities. International relations theory, as one of the primary mechanisms for translating the world into words, images and numbers, for translating the worded, imaged and enumerated worlds of different centers and peripheries in the world, cannot then avoid being either a part of the problem or an aspect of its resolution.[51]

Following Chakrabarty, one could argue that international relations, like many other disciplines, speaks, conceptualizes and theorizes the global through various "secular universals." Some secular universals such as power, ideas, state, sover-eignty, institutions, globality, governance, civil society and humanity constitute its core vocabulary. Though asserting uni-versality, these categories are also drawn or emerge frequently from the historical archives of Europe and the West. But the world is more than the "minor-ity" archives of Europe and the West, much more, and so any non-colonially oriented interna-tional relations is necessarily faced with the task of making these concepts travel beyond the European archive to spaces and worlds that are radically different; so different that the archival mode itself might be a border that needs to be crossed.

In analyzing the problem of the postcolonial scholar, Chakrabarty helps us to reject both the colonial orientation of the Eurocentric scholar and the cultural parochialism of the nativist backlash. Arguing that such secular universals are "indispensable but inadequate" in our contemporary moment, Chakrabarty directs our attention to the processes between different spaces and thus to a specific politics of translation between multiple "life-worlds" or, to follow Mignolo here, different "loci of enunciation." What would such a process of translation between different spaces, between multiple loci of enunciation, between here and there, between multiple images, look like?

I can only suggest the beginnings of an answer here.

After attending a lecture on the Spain-Morocco border, a colleague and friend emailed me a photograph taken by Javier Bauluz in July 2001. The picture shows a couple sunbathing on a beautiful shore in Zahara de los Atunes, an enclave of Spain in North Africa. Doubly-protected from the sun by an umbrella and eye-shades, relatively bare, the couple sits with their hands rolled around their knees and with a water cooler and some drinks next to them. In what appears, in the picture, to be only a few feet away, face turned away from them, hands seemingly curled behind, lies a clothed and black body fully exposed to the harsh glare of the sun. The body was that of a migrant who had died while trying to cross the ocean into this piece of Spain. There was some controversy about the angle from which the photograph had been taken and about its title: "The Indifference of the West."

It is a chilling photograph about the uneven protections and exposures different social bodies face as they attempt to navigate the spaces of international relations. But what I find note-

67

worthy about it, notwithstanding the controversy about the angle, is precisely the angle itself. Rather than separate the tourist's gaze from the gaze of the migrant and insulate both from me, the viewer, who is both tourist and migrant, the photograph sutures us all together and compels me to think about the relations connecting all three. Locked into that triangular relationship, I cannot but recognize myself as the accused as well as the accursed subject of international relations.

VIII

Colonial Presents

24 January 2009

"Barack Obama gave the go-ahead for his first military action yesterday, missile strikes against suspected militants in Pakistan which killed at least eighteen people. Four days after assuming the presidency, he was consulted by US commanders before they launched the two attacks. Although Obama has abandoned many of the "war on terror" policies of George Bush while he was president, he is not retreating from the hunt for Osama bin Laden and other al-Qaida leaders. ... The strikes will help Obama portray himself as a leader who, though ready to shift the balance of American power towards diplomacy, is not afraid of military action."[52]

30 January 2009

On Thursday, 30 January 2009, it was reported that the shoe-throwing monument had been removed by local officials, "a day after it was erected."[53] "The monument commemorating the journalist who hurled his shoes at President George W. Bush was taken down a day after it was erected, local officials in Tikrit told CNN. ... ...[T]he monument was removed after a request from the central government...."

8 July 2010

Gen. James Mattis has been joking recently that after forty-one years in the Marines, he was going to return to his home of Walla Walla, Wash., to become an onion farmer. He'll have to wait. The four-star general is going to Tampa, Fla., to take over for Army Gen. David Petraeus as commander of the US Central Command, overseeing combat in both Afghanistan and Iraq. The news was announced by Defense Secretary Robert Gates at a press conference today. Mattis now faces a Senate confirmation. … Mattis is also known for his mouth. He is a jokester in person and also blunt. In the spring of 2003, in the first of his meetings with recently defeated Iraqi military leaders he famously said: "I come in peace. I didn't bring artillery. But I'm pleading with you, with tears in my eyes: If you fuck with me, I'll kill you all."[54]

Associates of General Mattis offer an explanation for the contradiction of a general who uses "ain't" in public but devotes his government moving allowance to hauling a library of 6,000 books from station to station, forgoing most personal effects. He is a reader of philosophy who has patterned his speeches and writings on Aristotle's famous dictum on effective communications: Know your audience. When he is speaking to Marines, he speaks like a Marine. When he is speaking to defense chiefs or senior government leaders, he uses their language. And he is a reader of history. He was once asked which American Indian warrior he most respected. His answer was a tribe-by-tribe, chief-by-chief exposition spanning the first Seminole war to the surrender of the Lakota.[55]

3

PROPRIETY AND ATROCITY

I

Writing about the trial, in Turkey, of the novelist Orhan Pamuk for "denigrating Turkishness," columnist George Monbiot highlights the "anachronistic brutality" of Turkey's laws and the "staggering, blithering stupidity" of this course of action.[1] Comparing these measures of the Turkish government unfavorably with those of the Europeans, he draws attention to the "more effective means of suppression" that the latter have long had in place. Commenting on the ability of European countries to produce "an almost infinite capacity to forget [their] atrocities," Monbiot notes: "When a Turkish writer uses that word [atrocities], everyone in Turkey knows what he is talking about, even if they deny it vehemently. But most British people will stare at you blankly." Asked about British atrocities, they would have no idea what you were talking about, says Monbiot, even though there were multiple well-documented examples ranging from the between twelve and twenty-nine million Indian famine victims of colonial policy in the 1870s[2] to the more than a hundred thousand tortured or killed in concentration camps in Kenya in the 1950s[3] to the more recent cleansing of Diego Garcia.

The production of Britishness or Europeanness then, in contrast to Turkishness, is also generative of "an almost infinite capacity to forget [one's own] atrocities." We could, if we wish, read this as one more instance of a technology, social in this case, that non-European states have not yet "developed" adequately. Or, taking the spirit of Monbiot's suggestion more seriously, we could explore what exactly it is that facilitates this capacity to forget. How are some states effective at producing this capacity to forget their own atrocities while other states "fail" miserably on even that dimension?

Monbiot's contrast between ineffective Turkish and more effective British methods of marking atrocities offers us an entry into this question. Let us focus, for a start, on the dimensions he highlights: "anachronism" and "stupidity." Both refer, to some extent, to different ways of being on the outside: anachronism relates to the presence of "something out of time," "stupidity" to being on the outside of "reason." Both thus speak to certain dislocations, a certain out-of-focusness in relation to the socially dominant conceptions of time (history, memory) and reason.

It is, however, not the "incompetence" of the postcolonial (in relationship to the dominant conceptions) as much as the hyper-competence of the colonial in relation to the dominant conceptions that concerns me here. What goes into the effectivity of colonial memory, what processes produce and sustain the "in-focusness" that produces amnesia about colonial violence and atrocities in the colonizer?

If Monbiot's insight is correct, the capacity to narrate one's actions properly in the fields of time and reason differentiate effective from ineffective methods of marking atrocities in international relations. Colonial effectivity in generating amnesia about the self's violence is intimately related to colonial propriety: the ability to narrate one's "brutality" or violence in ways that are "well-placed," "situated correctly," and "socially appropriate" i.e. within the proper time (non-anachronistically) and/or within the proper context of reason (a context that does not appear to be "blithering" or "stupid"). The crucial difference then is not necessarily between the commission or non-commission of atrocities as much as of the effective or ineffective narrating of violence through appropriate rituals and proper protocols of explanation.[4] What then are some of the rituals governing the proper situating of atrocities in international relations?[5]

II

Narrating Atrocities in International Relations

Let us begin with an atrocity:

> In the wake of the relief of Lucknow, a young boy approached the gate to the city, supporting a tottering old man, "and throwing himself at the feet of an officer, asked for protection. That officer...drew his revolver, and snapped it at the wretched supplicant's head...Again he pulled the trigger—again the cap missed; again he pulled, and once more the weapon refused its task. The fourth time—thrice he had time to relent—the gallant officer succeeded, and the boy's life blood flowed at his feet."

This story from the annals of the 1857 revolt of Indian soldiers against the British is recounted in Niall Ferguson's 2003 book on the British Empire.[6] Ferguson has achieved some prominence in recent years by his strenuous defense of an imperial role for the US in the current international system. Basing his arguments on a positive account of the British Empire's role in maintaining "global order" and promoting capitalism, Ferguson represents a new breed of writers who have been at the forefront of attempts to resell imperialism's virtues to US policy-makers.

As the story above demonstrates to some degree, Ferguson's book does not directly deny or ignore some of the documented atrocities under British imperialism. But neither does it leave them unmarked. How, then, does it situate this atrocity and transform it into a defense rather than a condemnation of the British Empire?

After narrating the story Ferguson notes: "To read this story is to be reminded of the way SS officers behaved towards Jews during the Second World War."[7] In saying this, Ferguson recognizes the potential parallel that exists between British atrocities and the more pervasively acknowledged accounts, within the international relations imaginary, of Nazi atrocities. He thus raises the specter of a British colonialism that might have shared similarities with the Nazis' treatment of Jews. But he seeks to put that specter to rest with the assertion of a difference.

"Yet," he says, "there is one difference." "The British soldier who witnessed this murder loudly condemned the officer's action, at first crying 'shame' and giving vent to 'indignation and outcries' when the gun went off. It was seldom, if ever, that German soldiers in a similar situation openly criticized a superior."[8] This is the colonial defense, the British difference, then.

What separates a British atrocity from similar ones by the Germans is that another Briton "openly" voiced a protest. That Briton didn't act, at that moment, to stop the officer. He didn't risk his life or limb to save the life of the boy but he "openly" voiced, registered and recorded a protest. And that "open voice" is now narrated as an important moment in the proper re-telling of the original atrocity, a moment that is meant to distinguish one colonial identity from another.

Colonial Atrocities and the British Difference

Thinking from other voices, voices shut out in many ways—the voice of that "wretched" boy, the voice of the "tottering old man," the voices of the once colonized—the British difference from the Germans does not appear particularly striking to me. A Briton's protest, unbacked by action in that moment, meant little. But, clearly, from Ferguson's perspective, this was an important difference, a difference worth marking. How do we understand that?

I would argue that Ferguson deploys this moment to achieve a number of narrative effects in his broader defense of the British Empire. Two of those effects are of particular relevance to us here. First and foremost, Ferguson marks the difference between the British and the Germans in order to split the imperialist identity into two: a good identity and a bad one. Good imperialists are those who (in this case openly) record and register atrocities while bad imperialists leave little room for that. Good imperialists record and take note of dissent within. They are capable of correcting themselves, of improving their identity and of becoming better imperialists.

What is the significance of this within Ferguson's argument?

This distinction is important because it leaves unasked basic questions about the unjust social and political relationship between the colonizer and colonized—questions about the nature of imperialism/colonialism as a fundamentally unjust and authoritarian enterprise in itself; or of how one set of human beings (British or German or Belgian) could conceivably possess such arbitrary and despotic power over others (Indians and Jews and Africans)—and concentrates its attention on the narrower and more "technical" issue of how the colonizer can learn to behave in a better fashion towards the colonized. In other words, it replaces structural ethical and political questions with technical/instrumental issues of good and bad behavior towards others.[9]

Second, once the focus is no longer on the structurally unjust character of a colonial relationship, Ferguson can subject it to a seemingly neutral, instrumental analysis—tallying, what appears to him, to be its pros and cons—and coming to a "reasoned analysis" of what it achieves and what it doesn't. This cost-benefit analysis, in the end, forms one of the primary justifications, in Ferguson's account, of the overall virtues of British imperialism.[10]

Colonial atrocities and French identity

Let us consider another atrocity.

Describing the French colonial practice of waging a "total war" against the "rebels" in Algeria, the historian Douglas Porch recounts the following incident:

> The growing savagery of the war hit its nadir in June 1845, when Colonel Amable Pelissier trapped a group of Arabs in the caves of Dahra in the coastal mountains north of Cheliff. After desultory negotiations, Pelissier ordered a fire built in the cave mouth. Five hundred Arab men, women and children were asphyxiated. …Other mass liquidations followed over the next two years.[11]

Another account of this atrocity, Assia Djebar's *Fantasia*, places a higher number on the dead.[12] But number is not, for my purposes here, the most important point at the moment. I wish to ask: Does Porch leave this account of French colonial atrocity unmarked as just one more colonial atrocity or does he feel compelled to explain it to, locate it for, the reader? Following his story, Porch notes a compulsion: "It must be said…." What, I wonder, must be said after such an atrocity? What truth insists on being said and being heard following a description of the ugly killing of five hundred men, women and children? "It must be said," Porch says, "that the French behaved with no greater brutality abroad than did other colonial powers—the Russians in the Caucasus, the British during the Indian Mutiny, or the Germans at the turn of the century."

No greater brutality.

No greater brutality—not necessarily lesser brutality, but assuredly not more brutal than the Russians, the British or the Germans. Why must this be said? Why does Porch feel a compulsion to surround his account of French colonial atrocities by this comparative estimate of brutality?

Like Ferguson, Porch feels a compulsion, a compulsion to compare with others who did similar things. But Porch feels a compulsion to assert identity with these other colonial powers and their brutalities abroad while Ferguson felt compelled to mark a difference. Porch feels the need to say that the French were no different from the other Europeans.

It is crucial, once again, to note that Porch's assertion of identity in European colonial practices is not offered in order to build solidarities with the colonized, in order to offer a perspective that would be open to a better understanding of their suffering. Porch is not feeling compelled to say: Look, how horrible were the practices of colonial warfare! And isn't it a shame that all of Europe was engaged in this!

No. Porch marks an identity in terms of colonial atrocities not so as to condemn European colonial practices in general but primarily to establish the broader context for making "sense" of these practices. What he is, in effect, saying, feeling compelled to say here, is: "Let us think twice about condemning French colonial practices because they were no different from what other Europeans were doing. Condemn the French for this atrocity and you cannot but condemn Europe. Europe's hands are bloody. French hands are no bloodier." This is not so much a criticism of colonial atrocities as a preemptive taking of hostages to forestall condemnation.

Once again, this compulsion to assert an identity (or as in the case of Ferguson a difference) in European colonial atrocities, when considered from the outside—the perspective of the Ouled Riah tribe in this case, the tribe that was wiped out in the first fumigation, from the perspective of the Algerians, from the perspective of the once-colonized—is a meaningless difference, a nonsensical, even obscene, ritual of inter-imperial jostling. But Porch feels a need to mark the similarity. He does not feel a need, a compulsion, to view it, to narrate it meaningfully from the side of those asphyxiated or from the side of the Algerian women and children. He marks it from within the borders of colonial Europe, as if he were engaged in conversation only with, or afraid of the judgment only of, other colonial powers.

Porch then takes another step—a step similar to that taken by Ferguson.

Noting that these campaigns "outraged Frenchmen," he says:

> "It was only too obvious that Algerian service had distorted the values of French soldiers, and that a gulf had opened between the claims of France to bring civilization and order to Africa and the bitter realities of conquest. In 1846, Alexis de Tocqueville returned from Algeria horrified by the excesses of the military regime there—he later described the officers of the Algerian army as 'imbecilic.' The atrocities of the French army in Algeria, their flaunting of the most basic notions of liberty even when dealing with European civilians, fed anti-militarism in France that with the Dreyfus affair at the end of the century would become a significant political force."[13]

In thus situating the colonial atrocity, Porch secures it within a larger narrative of progressive French nationalism. Service in Algeria had "distorted" the essence of Frenchness in some French citizens but also "outraged" other French. This outrage then became the origin for a "significant political force" of "anti-militarism" within France. Yes, some French soldiers committed some terrible atrocities in Algeria. It must be said that these were no different from the atrocities committed by other European powers in their colonies. But these atrocities were also corrected by the French themselves, from within and, in fact, these led to some important political changes.

The story is thus embedded in a narrative where a threat of corruption is overcome and followed soon thereafter by redemption. Whatever unfortunate things might have happened to those Arab men, women and children who were smoked to death by French colonial practices, Frenchness, like Britishness in Ferguson's case, is redeemed by the outrage of the French themselves, as it is by the compulsion of Porch to say some things—some very particular things—after narrating an atrocity.

III

Propriety, Perversity and Atrocity

In October 2001, as the US was bombing Afghanistan, CNN's international correspondents received some instructions from their Chairman, Walter Isaacson, about what would be construed as "perverse" coverage of civilian casualties in the bombing.[14] Since perversity is a condition of "purposely being unreasonable" or "purposely deviating from what is accepted as good, proper, or reasonable," there might be some clues here to the protocols governing the proper coverage of international atrocities in the present.

Walter Isaacson, it turns out, had "ordered his staff to balance images of civilian devastation in Afghan cities with reminders that the Taliban harbors murderous terrorists." Noting, "it seems perverse to focus too much on the casualties

79

or hardship in Afghanistan," Isaacson said that "we must redouble our efforts to make sure we do not seem to be simply reporting from their vantage or perspective. We must talk about how the Taliban are using civilian shields and how the Taliban have harbored the terrorists responsible for killing close to 5,000 innocent people."

What are the rituals of perversity and propriety in covering civilian casualties then? Proper reporting should not be a simple act of reporting from "their" perspective or "their" vantage point. It must be reporting that "redoubles its efforts" to avoid reporting from "their perspective." It must be reporting that feels a compulsion ("we must talk about"), when talking about casualties there, to "remind" the listeners about the problematic character of the leadership "there" and its connection to the suffering of "innocent" people here. It cannot, it should not, "simply" report the suffering of people there. It cannot "simply" report their suffering. That would be "focusing too much on the hardship there." That would indicate a lack of balance. That would be perverse. Proper reporting ensures that viewers have a correct understanding of all the relationships that are necessary to make "sense" of civilian devastation or hardship in Afghanistan.

What would that correct understanding entail? It would be one under which, as Isaacson formulated it in an interview, "You want to make sure people understand that when they see civilians suffering there, it's in the context of a terrorist attack that caused enormous suffering in the United States."[15] That is, a correct understanding is one which sees suffering there as connected to the suffering here. Not in the sense that we here can/should sympathize with their hardship/suffering there but in the sense that if you are suffering there it is because of what your leaders did or allowed to be done to "5000 innocent people" here.

Isaacson's memo also asked that CNN, "in covering Afghan casualties," not "forget it is that country's leaders who are responsible for the situation Afghanistan is now in." That is, a non-perverse or proper coverage would ensure that viewers understood constantly that the responsibility for the hardship there arose not from the US bombing but from the actions of the Taliban leaders there. Clearly, while the actions of US leaders don't cast a shadow on the "innocence" of US citizens living in a representative democracy here, the actions of an authoritarian Taliban override any presumption of innocence on the part of Afghan civilians living in a theocracy.

Given the complex nature of some of these causal connections, CNN decided to take no chances and went on to operationalize the order by providing the proper, non-perverse, language that civilian casualties must be embedded within. Its head of standards and practices, Rick Davis, offered the following linguistic formats for CNN anchors:

> "We must keep in mind, after seeing reports like this from Taliban-controlled areas, that these US military actions are in response to a terrorist attack that killed close to 5,000 innocent people in the US" or, "We must keep in mind, after seeing reports like this, that the Taliban regime in Afghanistan continues to harbor terrorists who have praised the September 11 attacks that killed close to 5,000 innocent people in the US" or, "The Pentagon has repeatedly stressed that it is trying to minimize civilian casualties in Afghanistan, even as the Taliban regime continues to harbor terrorists who are connected to the September 11 attacks that claimed thousands of innocent lives in the US ..." Even though it may start sounding rote, it is important that we make this point each time.[16]

The structure of proper reporting about civilian devastation elsewhere is given by a series of "musts," a compulsive series that ensures that the event is embedded within connections that are oriented to produce a specific understanding of the event.

Whatever else this understanding might be, it is never, it should never be, it cannot be, a "simple reporting" of their suffering or hardship or devastation. It should not be from "their" perspective. That would be perverse. That would be "too much."

Sometimes, these repetitions, it is recognized, might sound rote. But that should not matter. What matters is that this point is made "each time."[17] "We must," a colonial imaginary intones as it begins to report on our atrocities and their casualties there, "remember that...." Occasionally, in order to avoid sounding rote, it might even say: "Yet....and yet, it must be said....there is one difference."

IV

Postcolonial Perversities

In 1984, as a graduate student in New Delhi, I watched horrified as postcolonial India's Congress government stood idly by as politically instigated mobs roamed the capital city seeking out and killing Sikhs. In 2002, the scene repeated itself in the Indian state of Gujarat. Politically instigated mobs sought out and killed Muslims in implicit alliance with sections of the state apparatus. In both cases, the ostensible reason setting off these pogroms was vengeance: the assassination of Mrs. Gandhi in the case of 1984 and the torching of nearly sixty women and children coming back in a train from the disputed Babri Masjid/Ram Janmabhoomi site. Some of the local media, concerned like CNN with context, did tell their readers that they should, that they "must keep in mind..." the contexts of the assassination and the torching of women and children as they sought to come to terms with these killings. And the nation's political leadership followed the same script. Rather than condemning the killings in 1984, the then Congress Prime Minister, Rajiv Gandhi, evoked an analogy with the destructive forces of nature ("When a big tree falls, the ground shakes"). In 2002, the BJP Prime Minister, Atal Behari Vajpayee, in asking "Who started the fire?" directed the blame for the subsequent killings on the perpetrators of the train massacre. His minions evoked the laws of physics ("For every action, there is an equal and opposite reaction"). The obscenity of these references to natural forces or physical laws in the face of such horrifying killings contrasted sharply with their insistence on being accorded all the dignities and proprieties of sovereignty when it came to the reactions of other states.

When other governments expressed concern over the killings in Gujarat, the Government of India (through the Ministry of External Affairs), was outraged by what it saw as "foreign interference" in domestic affairs, asserting, for good measure, "that India needed no lessons in secularism from the West." When, a few years later, Narendra Modi, the Chief Minister of Gujarat under whose watch the carnage was carried out, had his visa to the US revoked by the US State Department, the protests were shriller. Though it was a Congress government at the Center now, the government of India (and opposition parties including the Left) protested vigorously at the US action with many claiming that this was an insult to India, the Indian Constitution and Indian sovereignty. The official Indian statement saw the revocation of Mr. Modi's visa to the US as an "uncalled for" response that "displays a lack of courtesy and sensitivity towards a constitutionally elected Chief Minister of a state of India."

In responding thus, the Indian state demonstrated an imaginary that was not only morally impoverished and parochial but also colonially oriented towards its own citizens. If the citizens of India are being butchered on its streets and other states express concern, how is that concern understood as "foreign interference" by the Indian government? What exactly is "foreign" about that articulation? How is the expression of such concern "interference"? These claims make sense within an imaginary structured on the principle that only Indians have a monopoly on the governance, care and regulation of all human bodies inscribed as Indian within that space. That this control/monopoly cannot be questioned even when these bodies are abused, tortured or killed. So state propriety—"courtesy and sensitivity"—in the face of atrocities demands the silence of others when Indians kill each other. It also demands that others refuse to pass any adverse judgments or act in any way to curtail the privileges of those responsible for them if they should happen to hold elected office.

But in making such demands of other states, in asserting the rights and privileges of state sovereignty in the face of horrifying atrocities within, the Indian government betrays a lack of proper schooling in the rituals of proper colonial governance. It practices rituals that are colonial and parochial (or national) rather than those that are colonial and global. In that, it has a lot to learn from the West.

This lack of a coloniality that is global in its reach was evident in a couple of ways.

Rather than generating and disseminating a set of universal ethical norms against which it would read, measure and pass judgments on others (from nuclear to humanitarian issues to issues of "freedom"), it finds itself on the receiving end of others' universalizing judgments. This is particularly ironic since this Indian withdrawal from universalizing judgments has come at a time when it has sought to globalize different dimensions of its economy and society. So, paradoxically, an autarchic India, under Nehru, exhibited a more universalizing morality than the India that began globalizing its economy after 1991.

A post-liberalization focus on "national interest" and "pragmatism" has meant a less "moral/ethical" approach to political events at precisely that moment when the West has turned its universalizing "morals" into a force for global governance.

What we have then is a situation where the West finds itself commenting on and intervening on a variety of humanitarian affairs globally while being spared criticism from within India. Particularly ironic is the fact that, in denying Mr. Modi a visa, the US government cited the report of the Indian Human Rights Commission and not any of its own agencies. In other words, the US government showed itself to be acting to deliver on universal judgments that India had made on itself. Intentionally or unintentionally, this can be read as demonstrating a double deficiency within India. First, you confine yourself to understanding, judging and condemning only those atrocities that have to do with India. This might show sovereignty but it also betrays a lack of universality in the scope of your ethical vision. Second, you investigate and judge your atrocities but are unable to prosecute those involved. The US, on the other hand, relying on India's own judgment (not the US's—and so seemingly demonstrating a certain respect for sovereign India's ethical judgments) also shows itself to be a better governor in actually doing something about the guilty. The net implication from the perspective of colonial governance and its proprieties: Both of the states are sovereign and colonial in the international system but one is more global in its coloniality while the other is, at best, national. And sometimes, even on that national scope, states like India can do with some advice and lessons on coloniality from states such as the US!

Unlike the West, the Indian state finds itself, in recent years, refusing to extend its morality to encompass the actions of others (as Belgium, the EU and the US do in many ways), but it continues to find that others don't reciprocate. Rather than (like Spain or Belgium or Germany) having laws that claim universality for certain crimes (so that a Pinochet, a Kissinger or a Rumsfeld could be called to account), sections of the Indian elite host and fete Kissinger assuming that his "realpolitik" is what governs the world and should dictate Indian foreign policy.

Postcolonial propriety lies then in that desire to be autonomous/sovereign in one's actions at all levels of the nation. Hence the celebration of democracy, of dissent, of civil society and NGOs and the establishment of Human Rights Commissions. But its limitations emerge very clearly when those who perpetrate atrocities domestically or internationally are not judged, condemned and punished properly. A perverse space then opens up for those who are better versed in colonial proprieties to "intervene" as the guardians of a universal humanitarian ideology. The Indian state, like the Turkish one, might or might not need "lessons in secularism," but both definitely need better schooling in narrating their atrocities properly if they are serious about realizing their colonial potential.

4

ZOOLOGICAL RELATIONS[1]

Trent Lott, Republican Senator from Mississippi, on how to deal with illegal immigration at the border:[2]

> People are at least as smart as goats. Now one of the ways I keep those goats in the fence is I electrified them. Once they got popped a couple of times, they quit trying to jump it.

I

Reading Dr. Seuss

I am reading Dr. Seuss to my children: "If I ran the zoo."[3] If he runs the zoo, young Gerald McGrew promises to let out the boring lions and tigers and restock it with some new and exciting animals. These new animals appear to have unusual names, are exuberantly illustrated and seem, many a time, to reside in strange and mysterious lands. So out with the lions and tigers and in with "Gussets," "Gherkins," "Gaskets," "Gootches" and "Mulligatawnys."

In order to bring these new animals to the zoo, Gerald McGrew travels to strange lands and relies on various assistants. Some of his helpers happen to be, well, Princes from Persia. But while he scrupulously mentions the exact number of Persian Princes (eight) who will carry his baskets of strange animals, he claims to have no idea about their names. I wonder, as I read, if I should make up something, some proper names, for these Princes from Persia? But can I be as creative and zany as the Doctor?

It turns out, however, that the good Doctor is pretty nimble and has already forestalled me in some ways. Not only does he not name his Princes from Persia but he also implores his readers not to ask for them. Please don't ask him/Gerald McGrew their names. This is something he just doesn't know. Gerald McGrew, it appears, knows the names of all his exotic animals as well as the strange places in which they reside but not the names of his human helpers from those places. This does not mean that Gerald McGrew is totally clueless about his helpers. He does know, for instance, that when he's hunting in "the mountains of Zomba-ma-Tant," his helpers "will all wear their eyes at a slant."[4]

So while you may learn about strange and exciting animals that don't exist—Gussets, Gerkhins, Gaskets, Gootches, Mulligatawnys—what you will not learn about are the proper names of the human beings in these seemingly new and different lands. We don't know what their names are. Please don't ask. We don't need to know who they are. What we cannot but know is that they will carry our baskets or help us with the capturing and hunting of strange and wonderful animals and even have helpful tags ("wear their eyes at a slant") to enable us to identify them.

Tagging apart, what stands out more than anything else about Gerald McGrew's catching of new and different animals is that he says he is "fine" not just with capturing animals such as Mulligatawnys (a "beast that brave chieftains ride") but also with bringing back some of the chieftains too.[5] Some chieftains from these strange and different lands, brave as they might be, would do just fine for his zoo.

So if they run zoos, should we expect some chieftains in them too? Shouldn't we?

II

Ota Benga, a—

Ota Benga, a—, was brought from the Congo to be exhibited at the 1904 World's Fair in St. Louis as part of an "anthropology exhibit" with "representatives of other aboriginal peoples, like Eskimos, American Indians and Filipino tribesmen..."[6] In 1906, he was also displayed, for a while, in the Bronx Zoo. When some black clergymen objected to the exhibition, the Mayor of New York refused to meet with them or to "support their cause." This refusal earned him the approval and congratulations of the zoo's director, William Temple Hornaday. Mr. Hornaday, a prominent player in the history of the zoo and of American conservation, wrote to the Mayor about how this event would be recorded: "When the history of the Zoological Park is written," he said, "this incident will form its most amusing passage."

It is recorded that a few years later, in 1916, Ota Benga, the—, killed himself with a revolver. The record also shows that Mr. Hornaday was not at all "surprised by Ota Benga's suicide. 'Evidently,' Mr. Hornaday said, 'he felt that he would rather die than work for a living.'"[7]

Ota Benga, a—, emerged in the *New York Times*, and hence onto the record, once again, a few years ago. This time he appeared as an "episode," a "perfect illustration," the mark of a racist scandal from a different time, a "mistake" of a young institution, a "moment in time."[8] Ota Benga was something that you looked back at "with a mixture of regret and resignation."[9]

He is so "Unthinkable Now."[10]

III

Hearing the Unthinkable

August 2006, Lebanon

> High on the hilltop last month, in the attack on the convoy, Mr. Safe's car was hit as well, and on fire. His wife got out with their baby, Ahmed, and Mr. Safe pulled his father to safety, but his mother burned to death in the car. "I felt that human beings had no value," he said, sitting in a quiet hilltop garden, a bandage around his hand. "The human became like animals, like simple fish."[11]

July 2005, London

> "I saw an Asian guy," said Mark Whitby.[12] "He ran on to the train, he was hotly pursued by three plain clothes officers, one of them was wielding a black handgun." … "As [the suspect] got onto the train I looked at his face, he looked sort of left and right, but he basically looked like a cornered rabbit, a cornered fox." "He looked absolutely petrified and then he sort of tripped, but they were hotly pursuing him, [they] couldn't have been any more than two or three feet behind him at this time and he half tripped and was half pushed to the floor and the policeman nearest to me had the black automatic pistol in his left hand." "He held it down to the guy and unloaded five shots into him."[13]

Jean Charles de Menezes, a——, had come to London from Brazil. On 22 July 2005, on his way to work, he was suspected, followed, grabbed from his seat and shot to death in Stockwell Tube Station by London police. He was twenty-seven years old. Initial reports—about his running away from the police and wearing unseasonably warm clothes—turned out to be wrong. It also turned out that one of the officers suspected him on the basis of his "distinctive Mongolian eyes" while another couldn't identify him properly because he, the officer, was "relieving himself."[14]

There is no record of what Jean Charles de Menezes was thinking as he was grabbed from his seat and shot seven times in the head. Did he wonder about what was happening? Did he realize how history and the body, a very particular history, the history of his body—his "Mongolian eyes," his Asian look—and the body of history had conspired to betray him, fatally?

IV

Recording Some Notes on Camp

Navy Rear Admiral Harry B. Harris Jr. is the Commander of Joint Task Force Guantanamo. Responding to a query in the *Chicago Tribune* about what the US should do with the Guantanamo Detention Camp, Admiral Harris wrote an essay detailing life in that camp and the sort of responsibilities that befell him and other Americans.[15] He begins by taking issue with those in many "mainstream outlets" who had described the facility as a "prison camp." "Prisons," he points out, "are about punishment and rehabilitation. Guantanamo is about neither." It is "about the detention of unlawful enemy combatants" and about "the safe and humane care and custody" of all those held there.

Who are the people detained there?

"They" are "dangerous men associated with Al-Qaeda or the Taliban captured on the battlefield waging war on America and our allies, running from the battlefield, or otherwise closely associated with Al-Qaeda and the Taliban."

They are "committed jihadists and terrorists," "men who proudly admit membership at the leadership level in Al-Qaeda and the Taliban, many with direct personal contact and knowledge of the September 11, 2001, attackers."

They are "terrorist recruiters, facilitators, explosives trainers, bombers and bombmakers, Osama bin Laden bodyguards and financiers."

They are "enemies of our nation," "terrorists ...not represented by any nation or government," and "people who do not adhere to the rules of war."

Who are the detainers?

"We" are the "soldiers, sailors, airmen, Marines, Coast Guardsmen and civilians responsible for the safe and humane care and custody" of those detainees.

We are those who "aggressively look for ways to build on [this] 'safe and humane care and custody' mission...."

We are those who "provide" and "give;"

We "guard them, feed them and care for them." And we are those who even when the detainees take advantage of us, "exact" the "only retribution [we want]," viz. "to simply continue to serve with pride, dignity and humanity."

We are, among others, those "young Americans" who are "upholding the highest ideals of honor and duty in a remote location, face to face with some of the most dangerous men on the planet."

What is the nature of the conditions at the "detention camp"?

The Admiral's description of the conditions at the camp can be usefully divided into different headings ranging from physical infrastructure to food/shelter, religious and health facilities.

In describing the physical infrastructure of the camp, he draws attention to Camp 4, where "a large number of detainees live." This was, "a communal-living facility where they are housed in a barracks setting with access to 12 hours of recreation and exercise per day" with "ample exercise areas and equipment for them." If Camp 4 was not attractive enough then one could look forward to a new "Camp 6, a $30 million modern medium-security facility that will make life even better for the detainees, while adding safeguards for the troops and civilians who work here."

The Admiral notes the cultural and religious sensitivity to the Other that permeates the camp taking extra care to mention the additional financial burden this imposes:

> All detainees at Guantanamo are provided with three meals a day that meet cultural (halal) dietary requirements—meals which, incidentally, cost three times what meals for our servicemen and [service] women here cost. We fully meet special dietary needs (e.g. Type 2 diabetes, vegetarians, fish-but-not-red-meat-eaters etc.) of many of our detainees.

But realizing that detainees do not live by food alone, the camp also facilitates the practice of a different faith:

> Detainees enjoy broad opportunities to practice their Muslim faith, including the requisite calls to prayers five times per day, prayer beads, rugs and copies of the Koran in their native languages from some forty countries. Directional arrows pointing to Mecca have been painted in every cell and camp. The American guard force is specifically prohibited from touching detainees' Koran....When prayer call is sounded, the guards set out "prayer cones"—traffic cones stenciled with the letter "P"—for 30 minutes of prayer call, as a visible reminder for the guards to avoid noise and disruption.

Drawing attention to the secure and comfortable shelter that is provided, he observes: "We provide safe shelter and living areas with beds, mattresses, sheets and running-water toilets. We also provide adequate clothing, including shoes and uni-

forms, and the normal range of hygiene items, such as a tooth-
brush, toothpaste, soap and shampoo."

The medical facilities are simply "outstanding" and have
served to increase the life span of the detainees:

> We provide outstanding medical care to every detainee, the same
> quality as what our service members receive. We are improving
> the health and extending the life span of the detainee population
> in our charge. Last year, we completed building a $2.4 million
> camp hospital to treat detainees. To date, we have completed
> more than 300 surgeries, including an angioplasty, and more
> than 5,000 dental procedures. We provide eye care and issued
> almost 200 pairs of glasses last year. We have given nearly 3,000
> voluntary vaccinations, including diphtheria, tetanus, mumps,
> measles and rubella—in many cases they are the first immuniza-
> tions detainees have ever received—as well as treatment for hep-
> atitis, influenza and latent tuberculosis. We offer complete colon
> cancer screenings to all of our detainees who are more than 50
> years old, and a variety of medical specialists provide preventive
> and restorative care.

Detainees also keep in touch with the outside world through
letters and the reading of books: "Detainees have sent and
received more than 44,000 pieces of mail since February 2002,
and our fully staffed detainee library has thousands of books
and magazines for their use. Our library team just returned
from a book-buying trip, adding nearly 2,000 Arabic titles to
the library."

Given such facilities and "safe and humane care," given the
numbers and the various measures of care, how do those in
their care respond? The Admiral admits that the objects of this
care have not really reciprocated either the humane concern or
the selfless care. They have often tried to take advantage of
these humane measures. For instance, since the American
guards are not allowed to touch the detainees' Korans, some
detainees have sought to "use this restriction to their advantage by secreting messages, contraband and the like within

their Korans." Others, many, "persist in mixing a blood-urine-feces-semen cocktail and throwing this deadly concoction into the faces of the American men and women who guard them, feed them and care for them." Many others have also gone on hunger strike or have tried to kill themselves, sometimes in a mass fashion.

The nadir of this tasteless response on the part of the detainees occurred on 9 June 2006 when three of them—Manei Shaman Turki al-Habadi, 30, Yasser Talal al-Zahrani, 21, and Ali Abdullah Ahmed, 29—managed to kill themselves despite the best efforts of their custodians and care-givers to prolong their life span. They left behind suicide notes that could, potentially, throw light on why they would respond with such disgraceful behavior towards those who were in charge of their "safe and humane care." But what was written on the suicide notes remains hidden while it is left to Navy Rear Admiral Harry B. Harris Jr. to set the record straight. He said the suicides were an Al-Qaeda tactic. "They have no regard for life, neither ours nor their own. I believe this was not an act of desperation, but an act of asymmetrical warfare waged against us," he said.[16] Colleen Graffy, the deputy assistant secretary of state for public diplomacy, observed, "It does sound like this is part of a strategy—in that they don't value their own lives, and they certainly don't value ours; and they use suicide bombings as a tactic." "Taking their own lives was not necessary," she added, "but it certainly is a good PR move."[17]

V

Bringing Back Mulligatawny[18]

From *Hobson-Jobson: The Anglo-Indian Dictionary: A spice-box of etymological curiosities and colourful expressions*:[19]

MULLIGATAWNY, s. The name of this well-known soup is simply a corruption of the Tamil milagu-tannir, "pepper-water"; showing the correctness of the popular belief which ascribes the origin of this excellent article to Madras, whence—and not merely from the complexion acquired there—the sobriquet of the preceding article.

The sobriquet of the preceding article?

MULL, s. A contraction of Mulligatawny, and applied as a distinctive sobriquet to members of the Service belonging to the Madras Presidency, as Bengal people are called Qui-his, and Bombay people Ducks or Benighted.

Ducks? Hmmm....

DUCKS, s. The slang distinctive name for gentlemen belonging to the Bombay service; the correlative of the Mulls of Madras and of the Qui-His of Bengal.

And who are the Qui-his?

QUI-HI, s. The popular distinctive nickname of the Bengali Anglo-Indian, from the usual manner of calling servants in that Presidency, viz. "Koi hai?" "Is any one there?" The Anglo-Indian of Madras was known as a Mull, and he of Bombay as a Duck.

And how is Mulligatawny defined in the present?

mul-li-ga-taw-ny/mùllige tawnee/ (plural—nies) n. a spicy meat and vegetable soup originally from eastern India [Late 18thC. From Tamil milaku-tanni, literally "pepper-water."][20]

Koi—hai?

VI

Desiring the Unthinkable

Jamil el Banna, a—, British resident, father of "Anas, nine, Mohamed, eight, Abdul Rahman, six, Badeeah, five," and

Mariam, three, husband of Sabah Sunnoqrot, went "with a friend to set up a peanut processing plant in Gambia" in November 2002.[21] He is now a detainee in Guantanamo Bay where he is not charged with anything. The reporter visiting his family in London notes that: "Anas cries when the word 'daddy' is mentioned in class, whatever the context."[22] Now, Sabah Sunnoqrot tries to "make things up to the children by being mum, dad, auntie and grandma to them."[23] Paying attention to a different context, she says: "When I saw the pictures on TV of Abu Ghraib I couldn't help thinking that the same things could be happening to Jamil. Monkeys in the zoo are better off than the Guantánamo prisoners. At least people can visit the monkeys."[24]

VII

Visiting the—

Under a black and white photograph of show-cased animals, in the Royal Museum of Central Africa in Tervuren, Belgium, an opening paragraph points out that the animals in the "Mammal Gallery" of the Museum were, from at least 1910 until 1959, arranged according "to size; the white rhino, the giraffe, the okapi and other such mammals in the middle; while smaller antelopes, rodents, etc. were placed in the showcases at the side."

The next paragraph highlights the changes that this arrangement underwent over time:

> In 1959 this arrangement began to evolve. Now the animals were grouped according to their distribution in the savannah and forest biotopes of Congo. The dioramas were made by the staff of the Museum between 1959 and 1972. Max Poll, head of the department at that time and a skillful watercolorist, painted the backgrounds.

A third and concluding paragraph speaks to the usefulness of this collection:

> Since its foundation, scientists from around the world have visited the Museum to study the Congo reference collections. The Museum houses numerous type specimens, including the bonobo and the Congo peacock. On the basis of type specimens a species is described and given a name.

The Colonial Museum, the Zoo and the Camp institutionalize a shared desire, almost a need: the need to make visible, exhibit, maintain the specimens collected (the chieftains who have been brought back). But this need to display, to make visible, runs alongside the need to contain, to frame, that which is displayed, frame it in a way that that which is displayed does not escape the boundaries of that frame: run away, kill itself, spill over, move beyond the range of measure and surveillance. The specimen must be contained, must remain, within one's ocular and cognitive grasp. This desired structure of visibility and containment, best exemplified in the institutions of the zoo (when the other is alive) and in museums (when the other is dead), requires a distinctive approach to signs: a need to hide, to keep invisible the "founding violence" involved in making the specimen available for our grasp. So even as a surplus of signs is generated about the evolving nature of the arrangements (from size to distribution, from cages to pastures, cells to facilities) or about the riches, the treasures and the virtues of the institution itself, the signs remain quiet about how this was possible at all in the first place.

What cannot really be asked or answered properly (if asked) in this equation are questions about the original acts of accumulation, appropriation, seizure, capture, plunder, loot and rape. For the Royal Museum, the question that is under erasure is about the initial acquisition of its "treasures": How was that accumulation possible? How did these specimens, not native to Belgium, come into the heart of Belgium? How did Belgium get to house the Okapi, the Bonobo and the Congo Peacock, among others?

The zoo generates a surplus of signs around the uniqueness of the Okapi on display and its protection and stewardship of that species as well as the institution itself:

> Okapis are shy and solitary and are closely related to giraffes; sometimes called "forest giraffes." Every individual has a unique pattern of stripes on the hindquarters and hind legs, comparable to human fingerprints. The offspring recognizes its mother by the white stripes, but mainly these stripes provide the perfect camouflage in the jungle. Its very long tongue is a handy instrument to strip leaves from branches. They sometimes even use it to clean their eyes and ears! In 1919 the Antwerp Zoo was the first in the world to show this rare species to the public. Until this day the Okapi's pedigree is kept in the Antwerp Zoo and this is our important contribution to the preservation of the "forest giraffe." In the wild, the species is endangered due to hunting and habitat destruction.[25]

But it dare not, cannot, talk about the violent bond relating the two to each other and of Belgium to the Congo. Harry Harris wanes and waxes about the "facilities" at Guantanamo but is silent about the initial accumulation of captives: How were they acquired? What is the justice of that seizure? Such questions are deflected and deferred by the constant production of a seeming newness in the nature of the institution, the Camp, the Museum or the Zoo; seemingly new differences, new projects, new knowledge, new threats, new dangers, new ethics, new ways of saying sorry and yet continuing with the same:

> Zoos no longer bear any resemblance to animal collections of the 19th and 20th century. On the threshold of the 21st century they have developed into vital centres for the preservation of endangered animal species, as many of these have practically become extinct due to poaching, biotope destruction and pollution. ....

Intensive information and education campaigns in both our parks as well as international breeding programmes serve as tools for the preservation of many species. .... Scientific research in our animal parks and in the natural biotope support this type of nature conservation. ... Antwerp Zoo is in the process of constant renewal. The optimization of our animals' accommodation as well as the perception put across to our visitors require continuous improvements. That is why we welcomed the Thar goats and Takins into a mountain scenery, Spectacled Bears housed in a roomy exterior enclosure and 20 Nocturama cages now provide accommodation for 7 fabulous common quarters. Our Zoo has a so-called "living-collection," i.e. our animals will sometimes move to another animal park due to better accommodation or breeding programmes. As a result, you may not be able to see some of the animals at the indicated locations. We apologize for this inconvenience.[26]

We are not about just collecting animals anymore (as we/others were in the, presumably less enlightened, past; now we are on the "threshold" of the twenty-first century). Now, in this progressive now, we exude a virtuous vitality, one that involves us in protecting and preserving these animals as they are threatened, their very existence endangered (endangered by what? Should we assume those who populate and control zoos have little relation to those who poach, destroy and pollute? Or that the processes of pollution, biotope destruction and poaching are processes that happen over the heads or behind the backs of humans?) Nowadays, we inform, we educate, we breed, engage in research, optimize, conserve, renew ourselves, provide "fabulous common quarters" and, notwithstanding all this, are humble enough to apologize for our failings if we fall short in ensuring that you get a convenient view of these animals in their "indicated locations." We aim to optimize: "The optimization of our animals' accommodation as well as the perception put across to our visitors require continuous improvements."[27]

Is this perennial need to optimize, to optimize the relationship between the animals on display as well as the perceptions of the visitors, to structure and restructure the displays, to organize and re-organize the descriptions, arrange and rearrange, renew and make anew the camps, the zoos and the museums on seemingly ever more systematic and evolving grounds, ever more modern ways, only another way of blinding oneself to the more basic questions of violence and justice regarding the Other, to the always already present but framed and contained—?

VIII

Riddles: Who Am I?

From the pages of the booklet published by the Minnesota Zoo:

Animal Riddle:

Who am I?

Read the hints below and see if you can guess what animal is describing itself:

1. I live near the water, my teeth continually grow, and I chew lots of trees for food and shelter. I am a—

2. I like to eat many different things. I often come out at night when you are sleeping and go through your garbage. Sometimes you will find me washing my food before I eat it. I am a—

3. If you cross paths with me keep your fingers away! Although I move slowly I have a nasty bite and grow very large. I am a—

4. I have very beautiful patterns on my scales but sometimes people are scared of me because they think I bite even though I only do if I need to protect myself. If it weren't for me you would have a lot of mice eating your crackers, cereal and pop tarts. I am a—[28]

101

Am I an animal "describing itself" or am I an animal silenced, re-described and framed even as you throw my voice and pretend/perform my "I"? What role do my self-understandings play in your imagined understandings of my "I"? Do your riddles and resolutions, questions and answers (research puzzles?) engage my being, my understandings, or do they dig and fill holes in your imaginatively constrained and Other-containing productions of my worlds?

Who am I to you? Does it have anything to do with me, with us?

From the pages of the *Financial Times* (London):

Who am I?

Country Riddle

Global Domination Via the Back Door

Brussels blog (Tony Barber): —'s hunger for African raw materials is well-known. Less well-known, but utterly fascinating, are the stratagems which—uses to satisfy its hunger.

A few months ago, some officials from—were being shown around Belgium's Royal Museum for Central Africa, which is located in Tervuren on the outskirts of Brussels. Known for short as the Africa Museum, this is one of the world's great anthropological, zoological and geological institutes, with wonderful collections of ethnographic objects, insects and tropical wood as well as an active scientific research center.

The Africa Museum houses the archives of Sir Henry Morton Stanley, the Victorian Explorer who played a part in the annexation of what is now the Democratic Republic of Congo (DRC) by King Leopold II of Belgium. In addition, the museum has all sorts of detailed maps and geological data about central Africa in its possession.

Given the DRC's large reserves of diamonds, gold, copper, cobalt, coltan (used in mobile phones and laptop computers), zinc and manganese, this makes the museum a place of more than passing interest to mining executives, financial investors—and guests from booming economies in Asia.

So after a routine tour of the stuffed animals, the—visitors suggested to the museum staff that it would be an honor, a privilege, an unforgettable gesture of friendship, if they could be allowed to take a quick look at the maps and other specialized documentation not generally on public view. Of course, of course, came the reply. Why ever not?

So in they trooped into the vaults. Then the—put in another request. Sorry to be a nuisance and all that, but would it be possible to take some copies of these materials?

What happened next is difficult to pin down. According to one version of events, the offer of a €20 banknote was enough for the—to get their way. If so, it was—from a——point of view a brilliant and almost unbelievably, ridiculously cheap coup.

No need to send out geologists and surveyors to central Africa— it's all been done for you a century ago! And no need to dip too deeply into—$1,682bn foreign exchange reserves! Inflation may be preying on everyone's minds these days but, hey, €20 can get you a long way."[29]

Who am I?
a. Canada
b. China
c. US
d. Brazil
What am I to you?
Does it have anything to do with me, with us?

IX

(Study) Abroad at Home

Travel

The San Diego Zoo's Wild Animal Park is like no other place on Earth. Travel just 30 miles north of the Zoo and you'll find yourself in the middle of Africa, where more than 3,500 rare and exotic animals roam several expansive habitats as large as 100 acres. At the Wild Animal Park, you can hand-feed a gentle giraffe in the Heart of Africa® or catch a glimpse of rhinos, elephants and zebras while enjoying an excited guided safari train ride.[30]

That which is "like no other place on Earth" is still close to us, close enough ("just 30 miles north of the Zoo"), close enough to get us to "the middle of Africa" (a place so Other that it is like no other place?), to its "heart," the "Heart of Africa," (copyright protected), close enough to feed a gentle one or glimpse the not so gentle ones or take a safari ride. But even as you do that, even as we do that, even as we come so close to the "rare and exotic" Others, who or what are we finding? Is it, will it be, as the Park promises, ourselves at the center of all this, ourselves even in "the middle of Africa" (Dr. Livingstone, I presume?), and even as the Others (all 3,500 of them) roam all around us ("you'll find yourself in the middle of Africa, where more than 3,500 rare and exotic animals roam")?

How many others, how many more times, and in how many varied locations do we need to find ourselves in, in order to move beyond finding only ourselves? What manner of loss is this? What loss of manners, what disregard of the Others, does it constantly necessitate from us?

Wonder and Awe

Your involvement makes a difference! Como Park Zoo and Conservatory have been cherished destinations since the early 1900s. Millions have treasured the beauty of the flowers, plants and gardens in the Marjorie McNeely Conservatory. At Como Zoo, children and adults alike have enjoyed close encounters with gorillas, polar bears, tigers and giraffes. Each dollar you contribute will be carefully invested at Como Park Zoo and Conservatory to insure a future of awe and wonder for generations to come.[31]

Our involvement makes a difference. It allows us to "insure a future of awe and wonder for generations to come." But what is the source of this awe and wonder? How is it generated? By our ("children and adults") "close encounters" with "gorillas, polar bears, tigers and giraffes" and encounters which allow us to "treasure" the "beauty of the flowers, plants and gardens."

What is the nature of the "closeness" here? How do we come close, close enough, to wonder and be awed, close enough to treasure? We come close physically i.e. in terms of reducing the distance between us i.e. we are there, with them, close enough to see, touch, smell, taste and hear the Other. We can watch, maybe not touch (what if the other bites? Unless, of course, it is a "petting zoo" but then you have to wash your hands afterwards, disinfect them since who knows what these animals carry by way of diseases (well, we do and hence the precautions)); smell, maybe not taste, and possibly hear (though whether we understand their sounds/languages is a different issue). So it is this sort of a close relationship that engenders wonder, awe, an appreciation of beauty and care, above all care and concern of a certain sort (I mean, we want them to be well-fed and happy; after all, this is not a nineteenth century circus).

A close relationship that is the source of awe, wonder and beauty for us, one worth ensuring for "generations to come," but nothing here really comes in the way of a border, a frame, a wire, a moat, a line, an invisible (the more invisible the better) barrier separating the Self from the Other. It is this bounding that also ensures, testifies to and institutionalizes a fundamental asymmetry in the relationship, for generations to come: that even if the Other could also see us, smell us, maybe not taste us, hear us, maybe not touch us, it is never able to set the terms of our encounters.

Of course, it can withdraw and hide and sleep and refuse to see us... to some degree. But it can, as the song goes, never leave. It is always available to us—to (for?) our love and concern and care and affection and need for awe and wonder—but we are not similarly available to it. It lives in and is contained by our conceptual, institutional and emotional framework and our needs but we are not similarly constrained to inhabit or even negotiate the terms of this "close encounter" of our worlds.

I guess, unlike the others, we can come and go (to the zoo, the camp, the museum), talking of Michelangelo. Or should that be the other way round? We talk of Michelangelo and hence we get to come and go?

X

Talking Afghanistan

I see her as I come out of track thirty-three in Grand Central Station and head towards the subway entrance. Framed by a cover, she is on display in the window of Posman Books. I have known her for a while now, lived with her image in my head, seen her transformation into an adult, followed the torrent of words and emotions and actions that are said to have been launched in the wake of her face. In the international relations I study, she's my neighbor, a *padosi*, in a number of ways.

Though a neighbor, she is also a possession of *National Geographic*. Or, maybe it is because *National Geographic* owns her that we find ourselves coming and going in the same neighborhood. *National Geographic* displays her, circulates her, sells rights to her face and, of course, makes money off her, of her. Wherever she appears, she is exhibited under their banner. It is probably illegal, I suspect, to relate to her publicly without the consent of *National Geographic*.

It is through *National Geographic* that I also learn much about her global effect.[32] They tell me that since they brought her to light, countless people have been inspired to volunteer for humanitarian missions in Afghanistan, her home country. Inspired by what, you may wonder? Her face, her eyes, her looks: those who possess the rights to these also tell us that those aspects of her testify to the tragedy of her land. Drawn, it is reported by them, by the power of those "sea green eyes," many have begged *National Geographic* to tell them more about her life and her story: Who is she? Where did she come from? And more recently, where was she now? What had become of her? Was she okay? Care and concern pour out effortlessly at the sight of her face, of that cover with her face.

A quick question about that *National Geographic* cover brought nods of familiarity in my class. She was a well-known and inspiring image here. Asked what was so inspiring about her, one of the students cited her looks (Did he say looks or look? Does it matter?) as inspiring love in him. She is lovely, hence lovable. And how can one love her and not feel something for her country, for the place that birthed her, a place that could give birth to such a beautiful face? How cannot one appreciate then the passion for the lovable foreigner, that foreign passion, that love of a stranger, which she evokes in various passers-by?

National Geographic circulates her globally and it is to their narrative of her, a narrative of discovery, loss and revelation that I now turn my attention. What follows is her story, as articulated by them. It is, obviously, a "Special Report."[33] Could it be anything less for someone so inspirational, someone who's evoked such passions?

The story begins nearly a quarter century ago when *National Geographic* first discovered and displayed her.[34] She was known to them then only as "the Afghan girl." She came to their attention and hence, according to them, "face-to-face with the world," once again, around 2002. The Editor wondered if it was really her when he was told that the "Afghan girl" had been located again.[35] Stanley-like, a *National Geographic* "crew" had gone all the way to Pakistan searching for "the subject of the most famous picture" in the magazine's history. First displayed by *National Geographic* in 1984, her picture had been run by them on several covers including even a special collector's edition.

Yes, she was their most famous picture, a special collector's item, but why were they looking for her now? Well, for one, they realized that they did not know much about her after their initial capturing of her image. And then, second, there were all those concerned calls for more information about her.

Though, like Stanley, the crew did finally locate her, their discovery of her, unlike the case of Stanley's locating of Dr. Livingstone, only presented more problems, problems of establishing her identity and the truth of that identity (Dr. Livingstone obviously seems to have done a better job of standing out in the middle of a place that was "like no other on earth"). In the epistemically murky badlands of Pakistan and Afghanistan ("Stories shift like sand in a place where no records exist"),[36] how could they be sure she was who she might claim to be, the same person? This wasn't a simple meeting between two trustworthy interlocutors where only a handshake and a few words would suffice, even in the "heart of darkness." It was a more fraught and uncertain encounter between two contrasting cultures: one that covered its real in many ways and another that ceaselessly exposed them. In the former, stories shifted, records were non-existent, languages and looks were mediated, directed and diverted only through trustworthy relations on both sides. Simple handshakes and direct looks were out of the question there. This was not an encounter where three words (or, a name and a presumption) sufficed as an index of deeper affinities and solidarities.

But even if they couldn't believe their eyes or feel these truths through their hands, they realized they could "trust" her eyes, or rather the evidence of her eyes, which was already in their possession. Her eyes would now be examined more closely ("scientifically") in order to speak, symptomatically, to the truth of the rest of her body and of her being, thanks to a culture oriented toward the ceaseless exposure, the uncovering, of the real.

So along came the eye doctor... Along came the ophthalmologist who happened to be .... Pakistani. Could the crew stop with that? How certain could they be of her identity when the examiner was one of them? Of course, the Pakistani doctor is 100 per cent certain. But is his 100 per cent certainty the same as ours? Are we 100 per cent certain about his capabilities?

Of course, we recognize that one needs the locals to navigate the shifting sands, to conduct on-site investigations and collect concrete data, but can one ever be fully, truly, really certain of their qualifications or their capacities to draw general conclusions ("The qualifications of ... any native, could hardly be pronounced equal to such a task ["accustomed to generalization, and capable of estimating the value and drift of inscription and legendary evidence"], however useful they may prove as auxiliaries in such a train of research")?[37] Don't the discerning readers of *National Geographic*, readers with a critical eye, require more by way of certainty?

Onward then to more tests, more checking; let's double-check, especially the checker. Let us, in the interests of truth and validity and the historical record (one that would stand the test of time and not shift with the sands), move away from the badlands and back to the stable terrain, the firm ground, of institutes and institutions and subjects (critical eyes/I's) that are better accredited, socially and technically. So, Harry Quigley, an ophthalmologist at the Wilmer Eye Institute in Baltimore, examines the pictures of her eyes and confirms that it is the same Afghan girl. The same Okapi! Check one. Check two and check three are provided by a FBI forensic examiner and a Cambridge University professor.

Check. Check. Check! A triple whammy! Specialists from three different sites (clinic, crime branch, Cambridge?) back up the findings of the native! Not only do they corroborate the findings but they are also drawn into the wondrous nature of the process itself wanting to know more about this person and asking when *National Geographic* will reveal what happened to her. And so an invitation is extended to all of us, "all of you who've wondered over the years," to "turn the page."[38]

Turn the page, friends.

XI

When Steve Met Sharbat

The story of the *National Geographic* photographer Steve McCurry meeting the Afghan girl, Sharbat Gula, is narrated as a story of two memories. Sharbat's memory (as presented by the editor) is of anger at being photographed by a stranger. What the photographer remembers, however, is the softness of the light in a refugee camp that was "a sea of tents." He also remembers a shy girl who tells him he could take her picture. Left un-translated is the disjuncture between the two memories before us: her anger at being photographed by a stranger against the stranger-photographer's claim of her consent to being photographed. If she agreed to be photographed, why is she angry? How do we understand her anger or the disjuncture between the two memories?

In addition to the narrative privilege of leaving some things unaddressed, such as Sharbat's anger, the stranger-photographer and his crew claim the privilege of education. Sharbat Gula has "sea green eyes," we are told, but there is no "light in them."[39] My neighborly solidarity compels me to ask: Who exactly is the un-enlightened, uneducated (or uncultured?) one here? Sharbat Gula, with "sea green eyes" but no "light in them" or the stranger-photographer with powerful lenses and an eye for the "softness of light" but not for the glaring anger of an Other?

The *National Geographic* crew claim also the privilege of a superior knowledge in the relationship: of knowing Sharbat Gula and her "tribe." They tell us that she is Pashtun and that means that she comes from the "most warlike" of Afghan tribes, a tribe that is peaceful only when it is waging war. Steve also claims to know that girls from Afghanistan who were "just a few years away from disappearing behind a traditional veil, might be reluctant to have their picture taken by a male Westerner."[40] It is presumably this superior knowledge of Pashtun tribes and reluctant Afghan girls that takes Steve the stranger, Steve the educated Westerner ahead, and tells him exactly what to do next. "So," he says, "I proceeded carefully."[41]

But Steve, the educated, why proceed at all? Why not stop? Can't you see the anger, feel the reluctance? Why seize what is not being offered? What ethic of care is involved in "proceeding carefully?"

Why doesn't your superior knowledge of them, your better education, the light in your eyes (but not in hers), tell you to stop, to proceed no further, to respect that reluctance and to turn away from taking a picture that provokes anger at the very first glance? What journalistic culture, what photographic veil, stops you from respecting that reluctance, rather than seeking to overcome it through a careful procedure? What blinds you to an ethics of care, an ethic of turning away from an unwilling subject rather than quickly producing a careful procedure for looting it?

Reading the Face of History

National Geographic tells us many other things about this encounter.

We are told that in the eyes of the Afghan girl, we can see and read the tragic story of Afghanistan itself, the story of a country suffering twenty-three years of war with a million and a half killed and a few million more made refugees. We are told that her life-story is one of hardship, a hardship that has been particularly detrimental to her youth and that this story of hardship is common to many in Afghanistan. We are told that that much of her condition and her country's tragic history of a quarter century can be traced to the Soviet invasion, an invasion that also killed her parents. We are warned that we cannot turn away from the disturbing challenge her eyes pose for us.

Our Amnesia, Our Desert Sands Where the Stories Shift

We are not told this, but what if we read her eyes and are not really able to see what should haunt us but only manages to escape us: What if her eyes were saying to us, "You did this to me. You brought me to this state and now you are photographing me! How dare you?" What if that was the cause of her anger?

We dare not think this but what if the story of Afghanistan in the last few decades is also our story? What if, "proceeding carefully," it is impossible to think of that story without thinking of the US in that story? Is that destruction that killed so many and destroyed so many others' lives all the doing of the Soviets only? How does an "American" manage to make himself and his *National Geographic* crew invisible in the history of a war so intimately implicated in Cold War rivalries in Third countries? How do you turn away from those stories that her eyes may be blazing forth? What do we need to forget, Steve, to be disturbed but not really disturbed enough to look critically within? And if we do turn away from that challenge, what veils do we have to cover our face, what mechanisms to extinguish the light, what colors to conceal our shame at that moment? But we don't really have to turn away, do we? We are safe, aren't we, as long as we can claim the transcendent power of love, of our love and care and concern for the Other, for—?

As the story winds down, Steve tells us:

> I'm relieved to know that this young woman has survived and has been able to carve out a life for herself. I hope that finding her will be a good thing for her and her family. I'd like her to look back in ten years and be happy this happened. I intend to check in on her for the rest of my life. ... Afghanistan has been in a Dark Age for two decades. That she's resurfaced now is perhaps prophetic, a hopeful sign. We'll have to wait and see.[42]

I think Steve is onto something.

I am very relieved too. I see her now all the time. That's a hopeful sign, maybe even a prophetic one. She is ours, forever present, made available to be displayed, checked and maintained. I saw her just the other day in the Borders near Penn Station. She seems to be doing well; still glaring, of course, her sea-green eyes still inspiring, moving me, making me feel something powerful for (Is it love? Is it care?) whatever place, however dark, she might be from.

I wonder what NGOs operate in Afghanistan.

XII

Padosi
Not the slant
Of sea green eyes
But our colors
Betray you
Yellow-dull
Kulcha-naan lives
Halal red sickles
Sky-blue and white raptors
Or reapers?
Shower desert weddings
with
misty pink rain
The Bodhisatvas way laid
A mottled grey
Purple burkhas hug
Sandy brown bodies as
NGO-white tents crutch
Oddly-sawed ones passionately
Not the taunt of darkness
But the slits of our I's
the slants of our stories
Carve you
As I too raging red
Softly
Lovingly
Betray you, my sister

XIII

Save the—

Would you fancy being my godmother or godfather?

Handsome young animal, nice figure, beautiful eyes. In short, a good-looking stud, is looking for a nice godfather or godmother. Meet me at the Zoo. For one year, you pay the food costs. The Zoo provides a certificate for tax purposes in Belgium! For further information:....[43]

The Good God

Godparentship

Would you like to become a godfather or godmother of one or more of our animals? Then the "Animals Godparentship" formula could be ideal for you. Godparentship is available for all our animals, provided they are not taken yet: birds, mammals, reptiles, amphibians, fish and even a number of invertebrates. The contribution depends on the species and the godparent pays the feeding costs of one (or several) animals during one year. This support is an active input for the Antwerp Zoo and Planckendael objectives and is rewarded with a magnificent certificate with your godchild's picture, a tax certificate* plus the godparents name mentioned on a sponsorship sign in the Zoo. Become a godparent from 125 euro or more.[44]

5

HUMANITARIANISM AND ITS VIOLENCES (WITH BUD DUVALL)[1]

I

The Care of the Self: Contextual Sensibilities[2]

Yesterday, 21 February, we were part of a group of a few professors and nearly forty students participating in a student organized dorm discussion on "Censorship and Offensive Material in a Global Context." As the discussion began with questions of materials that were or could be seen as offensive, racist stereotypes, revisionist history, terrorist self-presentations, cartoons were all brought up, in fairly nuanced ways, as materials that were likely to be read as offensive. Once the discussion of terrorism picked up steam, the conversation turned to 9/11 and the ways in which US citizens rallied around each other after that attack. The question then came up whether, in the face of an attack that was condemned by many people in the world, there was something, anything, problematic about US citizens asserting themselves primarily as "American" at such a crucial moment. Did anyone find that nationalist bounding offensive in that moment? Silence. A long silence interrupted by one woman, a fresher, who said that that issue had been bugging her for a long time.

It is important to understand the audience here. These are mostly middle, upper-middle class students who see themselves as broadly left, if not radical. Many of them, especially if they are seniors, tout their Foucaults, Heideggers and Agambens quite proudly and exhibit a particular self-possession about their worldliness and cosmopolitan orientation. Darfur, nowadays, is not very far from their lips. We say this not to be dismissive about the self-presentation of these students but to highlight the fact that these are not those who would, typically, think of themselves as limited in their cosmopolitan sensibilities by the borders of any nation. They are those who are horrified and scandalized by a foreign policy defined by Abu Ghraib and Guantanamo. And yet, what seemed normal (one of the more articulate ones even used the term "natural") to them at a particular moment of vulnerability (a vulnerability that cannot but be situated in a global politics), was a bonding, an identification, at the level of their national community. It is not necessarily this national bonding that directly concerns us here. It is the more insidious issue of what differentiates their imaginations of the world in the context of caring about themselves and caring about others. Is their humanitarianism/openness to the other more evident when it is the injured other and relatively reticent when it is an injured self? Why are they not humanitarian in all moments of injury? Why are they not global in the case of an injury to the self and attentive to the other's local/national in the case of an injury to the other?

II

The Care of the Other: Does Context Matter?

"Horror, but no context" is how David Rieff[3] characterizes the nature of events in what he calls "humanitarian-tragedy

land."[4] Rieff points this out in discussing the role of the minor-
ity Western spectator whom he sees as the quintessential agent
of humanitarianism. It is in consuming these tragedies that this
privileged actor is moved from watching a spectacle to action
and intervention in order to stop the unfolding horror. This
foregrounding of horror occurs with the simplification of a
political story into a morality play where the "victims are
always innocent, always deserving of the world's sympathy, its
moral concern, and beyond that, its protection, even if that
means killing in the name of that protection."[5] Following
Rieff, we believe that it is not horror alone that appears without context before the humanitarian self. The care of the
Other, we would argue, is structured as a space in which compassion, assistance, aid, action and intervention all emerge
without an engagement of the specificities and particularities
of the local. The local is evacuated of all its particularities as it
takes its place within a universalized economy of passion, care
and activism. What impels action, what brings about a "moral
imperative to act"[6] is the vision of the injured, bleeding, dying
body of the Other. That is all we are assumed to need to know.
That is all that matters.

The injured bodies of the Other dominate the humanitarian
gaze. They are what get placed at the fore in our dialogues
with them. Between our criticism and their altruism lies suspended many an injured body. They bleed. They are malnour-
ished. They hover between life and death and glare at you.
"How can you not do something?" asks the humanitarian of
us. "This is an emergency. People are suffering, people are
dying." In "humanitarian land," the appearance of the Other,
their sighting, is always an emergency. It is the very condition
of their visibility within our community. And their visibility,
their emergence on the horizon of our community, is always
already the moment of action and not dialogue or critique.

Bodies in pain on the horizon! The pain of the Other, their pain, sets off a frantic race in time. They are dying! Let's do something. Place your fingers on the carotid. You can save them.

We find ourselves summoned.

Do we witness them only when they have to be saved, only when they are in a crisis, a critical stage? Can the Other make its appearance only as an emergency? Is it always an emergency when it appears on our horizon? What happens once the Other is saved? Does it move back into its invisibility?

We do not want them to die. But do we really care how they live?

III

Protesting Compassion

We protest. In the name of multiply muted bodies that will never be heard within this global economy of care. Surely, we argue, these bodies might be injured but they are not voiceless. What about engaging them as political beings, understanding their politics, their contexts and their conflicts? What if they could be the co-authors of their care? What role for democratic engagement and not administration or governance alone within the humanitarian economy?

We are chastised. Our questions and criticisms, we learn, are cynical, academic moves that are concerned with theoretical themes and not practical issues. They delay action, defer necessary interventions. They waste crucial time, energy and resources. They are debilitating of the altruistic efforts of well-intentioned souls. Between the critical needs of dying bodies and the noble intentions of self-less souls, who are we to come in-between? Shamed ever so subtly, we avert our eyes from the humanitarians in the room. We lower our voices and mutter to each other: Is there no space for the academy, for democracy, in the kingdom of humanitarianism?

IV

Learning Politics

We learn. We learn that it is not democracy that is the stranger/foreigner in the kingdom of humanitarianism. It is politics. Humanitarians, we are repeatedly told, are self-consciously neutral. They keep a distance from all political issues. Though the body in pain summons them to witness, to charity, to service, to save the other, there is nothing there, we learn, that can be soiled by the touch of the political. Humanitarian politics, we repeat after them, is a politics of neutrality. Neutral humanitarians! Is that possible? The title of a photocopied article of Charles Taylor hovers in our head: "Neutrality in political science." How academic of us? We chastise ourselves for having improper thoughts and resolve to do better.

Isn't neutrality in politics possible if the self can transcend the local, if the self is somehow above the local? Are we talking about humanitarian transcendence now? Maybe an Archimedean position, a God's eye view/gaze upon the world?

Maybe Google Earth?

V

Outrage

Zoom into Afghanistan. June 2004.

MSF is outraged.[7] Five of its workers have been killed there. MSF withdraws from Afghanistan blaming the political actors

121

on the ground for not ensuring a safe and secure framework for the actions of its aid-workers.

We share that outrage.

But doesn't that mean that MSF's actions also depend on the political; on the willingness of various actors in the conflict to be respectful, indifferent or tolerant enough to constantly allow them to make space for their actions. How can humanitarian neutrality not be a political production?

Maybe it is, say wiser others in the humanitarian kingdom. Let us rethink our relations to politics. "Politics can be a Madonna or a whore," says one of the more eminent practitioners of humanitarianism.[8] Politics as nurturing and virtuous motherhood, sin and temptation clouds our impiously secular minds; the humanitarian as a heroic masculine self empowered or corrupted by politics as woman. Jesus! Do we really have to go this way? We learn that the distinction between virtue and sin is not inherent to politics as woman but hinges on whether she helps or impedes the noble work of the humanitarian self. Are we back to transcendence, once again? Is humanitarianism on top now?

VI

Missionary Positions

We are haunted by a story, a scene from Tzvetan Todorov's *The Conquest of America*.[9] The setting is that of a massacre of Indians by the Spaniards. Las Casas, the Christian, is chaplain to the troops and a witness to the massacre. Enter a dying native, intestines falling out from a Spaniard's cut. Las Casas narrates:

> The Indian, moaning, takes his intestines in his hands and comes fleeing out of the house. He encounters the cleric [Las Casas]...

122

and the cleric tells him some things about the faith, as much as the time and anguish permitted, explaining to him that if he wished to be baptized he would go to heaven to live with God. The poor creature, weeping and showing pain as if he were burning in flames, said yes, and with this the cleric baptized him. He then fell dead on the ground.

We feel a sickness in our stomachs as we read that the priest reaches out not to gently push the intestines back but to talk about faith and baptism.

What did the Indian want? Was it the guarantee of an entry into heaven? Perhaps. Maybe the priest understood the Indian and his needs very well. Maybe that's what his "yes" conveyed. But we can't help wondering if Las Casas shouldn't, at least, have listened more than he talked? Is the presumption of the Indian's needs for our heavens and our Gods always enough? Are the humanitarian needs of the Other always already foretold somewhere? In a word? In a book? On TV?

In the mindful crossing of one self rather than in self-transgressive listening?

There are other critics of humanitarianism.

David Rieff,[10] for instance, in analyzing the crisis of humanitarianism, divides its world into two. There are those, a tiny majority, privileged enough to watch these disasters unfolding on TV and a vast majority that are condemned to live them. Rieff talks to (and sees himself as) one of those privileged enough to watch TV: takes himself and them to task, laments the shortcomings of this enterprise and points out a number of instances where they got it wrong. David Kennedy takes a more academic and more scholarly orientation.[11] Systematically self-critical, whether on an aircraft carrier or in an Uruguayan prison, he's scathing about spring-break activists and human rights missions.

The two texts are insightful enough to deploy in our classrooms as a corrective to/for those very students who don't trip over words like Darfur. For classes in critical international relations and introductions to international politics.

Both Davids take their worldly divisions for granted. Activists move from one world to the other, experience failure, fatigue, heartbreak and come back to discuss these. Both Davids point sensitively to all the limitations of their global missions and yet...and yet....

David Rieff meets an Afghan child whose father had been killed by an American bomb and wonders if his support, on humanitarian grounds, for the war had made her an orphan. He listens. And as he listens to her, "it was as if [his] opinions were in one universe and her experience in another."[12] He does not know how to cross that divide between the "universe" of his "opinions" and the "universe" of her "experience." David Kennedy paints the "darker" sides of his world's virtuous actions, but nothing about this courageous self-criticism comes in the way of seeing himself and his fellow activists as "rulers." What is needed, he pleads, is responsibility in our "rulership." He urges us to "rethink our humanitarian traditions as the search for grace in governance."[13]

The Kingdoms of the Davids take the sovereignty of the humanitarians in our world for granted. They reinstate rather than unravel the distinction between First World Sovereigns and Third World Subjects, between those with "opinions," "consciences" and "knowledges" and those with "experiences," "injuries" and "bodies in pain." Do Virtue, Truth and Power all exist only in one of these worlds? Is it primarily a question of constantly and self-reflexively rearranging the relations among these within one world: challenging Truth to speak to Power, Grace to flirt with Governance and Virtue to recognize its darker dimensions?

What do you think our darker sisters and brothers would say to such propositions? How would that Afghan child/

orphan theorize the "opinions" of a Rieff, son of Sontag, as well as the relationship of such opinions to her contemporary condition? Or the easy assumption of a global rulership by a Kennedy?

VII

Offensive Practices

Talk of two worlds, of Truth and Virtue and Power, reminds us of another of our darker cousins: Fanon.

"The colonial world is a Manichean world," Fanon intones.[14]

We nod.

"For the colonized subject, objectivity is always directed against him."[15]

We nod again.

"The colonized, underdeveloped man is today a political creature in the most global sense of the term."[16]

Amen.

What happens to these darker knowledges of the natives within the global economy of humanitarianism?

How would we rethink humanitarianism, if we fore-grounded the structural violence of a colonial condition rather than the dying bodies of the colonized?

In a colonial international system, does governance with grace suddenly cease to be the rule of one world over another?

Can the relationship of graceful rulers with degraded sub-jects, of those endowed with knowledge and conscience with those burdened by experience and suffering, can that relation-ship of transcended selves with battered bodies be anything other than political?

In a colonial system that stifles/kills/chokes the colonized at multiple levels, what does it mean to vehemently deny the political nature of the dying in the name of a humanitarianism that celebrates its own globality?

Can that humanitarianism and its claim to globality, its monopoly of a certain universality, be anything other than an offensive practice? (Maybe, you could demur, not as offensive as the direct conquest itself but offensive nevertheless...)

What form of analytical/conceptual censorship is it, then, that refuses to read humanitarianism as always already a political, and therefore potentially, a hegemonic practice?

6

POSTCOLONIALITY AND INTERNATIONAL POLITICAL ECONOMY[1]

I

Colonial Borders

I want to begin with a recognition and a deferral.

I recognize that critical analysis in IPE strives to move from the superficial to the deep, from appearance to reality, from the realm of ideology to that of truth. This essay, however, will remain, resolutely, at the level of the superficial, at the level of appearances, of masks, maybe, you might even say, inside of ideology. But I feel a need to defer the search for truth, for deep structures, and to spend some time thinking about what masks truth, and what it feels like inside the ideology that might ostensibly be shaping me.

So, a recognition first and then a deferral. Then to the realm of appearances, of ideologies, of masks, of what is visible and tangible.

The masks that intrigue me are the appearances of wealth, the superficialities of the "facts of richness," the facades of development, the veneers of advancement, the surfaces of places read through IPE and, by contrast, those relegated to

Development. In talking about these appearances, or the lack of them, I am speaking—or struggling to speak—from the space of those who typically cannot wear these masks, fall short in terms of these facades and spend whole lifetimes trying to keep up these appearances, achieve these superficialities, reach these surfaces—those in spaces studied by development studies, those in places trapped by the category of "underdevelopment," those not visible in or from spaces read by IPE.

Now we all know the problems with descriptions of spaces through the categories of development and underdevelopment; we know the critiques of teleology as well as the depiction of lack. Let us not tarry there because I am willing to grant that we are all post-all that, in theory.

Let us not tarry there because I want to linger elsewhere, on some other borders, some other divides—those between IPE and Development Studies, borders that are quickly crossed and denied from one side, from this side, but not so easily deniable or crossable from the other side.

Pausing here, as an aside, I also feel compelled to make explicit the seemingly little issues, the ever-so-trivial, that are not always obvious on one side of the border but are perennial and persistent sources of anxiety and tension and worry on the other side.

Let us take a minor example.

Many of you, given the nature of this audience, are familiar with the problems of organizing student and faculty study tours. Most things fall into place quite quickly except, as you will recognize, the students and faculty on the trip who happen to have passports from the places that are not, broadly speaking, studied under IPE but under Development. Those aliens, we know, need to plan earlier, think of longer lead times, and prepare to be stopped, questioned and possibly turned back or refused entry at the divide. It doesn't matter whether they are faculty or students, resident aliens or F-1s. Those passports contain words that chop, cleave and concentrate them into a different temporality; the signs on those pages betray them as provincial bodies whose stays can only be provisional. There is a divide then that appears as soon as one wishes to organize a study abroad—a border that also straddles the study of these two fields.

This is a fiction that is real, a fiction that is visibly constitutive of these two spaces.

There are other fictions.

I remember, quite vividly, as a graduate student, a couple of decades ago, stepping from the domestic into the "international" space of Indira Gandhi International Airport in New Delhi. The difference in what I would subsequently learn to call the "built environment" was tangible, palpable and intense. I could see it, sense it, smell it, touch it—I could apprehend the materiality of that difference, the significance of the line I was visibly stepping across. The change in colors (I remember the space of the international as painted in hues of light green), the change in texture (soft and seamless), the change in the sense of being enclosed (I had suddenly stopped sweating from the hot midnight Delhi air), the onset of a sense of being wrapped up and cuddled protectively as well as the sudden opening up of beautifully lighted lounges with enough places for all of us to be apart from each other.

The world widened as I crossed the border from Development into IPE. The crowds barricaded on the other side suddenly disappeared even as specific individuals came into view on this side. Everything seemed possible for a suddenly self-aware "I"—time, space and leisure. I could stretch. I could write. I could shop.

Desires that had till then manifested themselves primarily on glossy paper were now neatly suspended around me. I couldn't afford those desires yet but what till then was only an imagined possibility was suddenly material reality. Before, those strange colored bottles were images and ideas. Now they were tangible possibilities, the shapes of my realizable futures.

What I could now see was the material horizon of a different world as well as a different understanding of the political economy of this world. What I had begun to forget, begun to leave behind was a tangibly darker world. Outside, I remember leaving the night, harsh yellow lights, crowded taxis, sweat, un-conditioned air and friends and relatives. That world was becoming hazier materially, difficult to see.

I was crossing this border because IPE had crossed into Development earlier on in my life.

II

Masks, Magic and the Lightness of Wealth

Appearances, superficialities, visions, ideologies, once again—

As a school kid, in the 1970s, I remember my uncles and my cousins coming back to India from their jobs abroad. Doctors in Michigan and Mashad, they were on their annual visits home. But it did not really matter where they were coming from—whether it was the United States or from Iran—or what they did there. A number of things masked their presence in Hyderabad. Their return solved local problems in ways that the locals really couldn't. They could get telephones allotted, scooters sanctioned, real estate set aside. Moreover, they also always appeared fairer and younger. Their skins were smoother and, believe me, seemed whiter. Their overall bearing was necessarily lighter.

Welcomed by well-credentialed but under- or unemployed cousins, they would be received, warmly and tearfully embraced, and escorted back from the airport. Stories would pour out; so would colorful photographs of her/him standing in front of a large house within a green square, perched above a waterfall, playing in the snow, dancing at dinner parties; pictures of leisure and play and recreation and work in a world of well-demarcated lines, vivid signs, gainful and satisfying employment and, always, plentiful objects, a myriad magical things.

Eventually, it would be time for some of these magical things, these things that always had a capacity to evoke wonder and surprise, to make their appearance too. After a suitable interval, when the guests had relaxed and washed up and caught up emotionally with some of the more urgent events—who had survived and who had passed away, who needed to be mourned, who was newly born, newly married and awaiting celebration—the suitcases would be opened and the signs and fragments and wonders of the new world of IPE would tumble out. These wondrous beings would have their own stories to tell—often narratives of daring—because many of them were either illegal or alien in the world of development. They needed to be sourced in from the world of IPE under heavily policed conditions (not surprisingly, the kith and kin network on both sides of the colonial divide regularly watched the annual budget carefully to see which magical items could be trafficked into the country under what cover) but their smooth or safe arrival could never be taken for granted.

IPE spilled out the mundane and the marvelous with equal ease: red pencils with golden tips, pens that flowed flawlessly, T-shirts in strange colors with stranger slogans, pistachios, dried fruit, dark cloves, rich raisins, generic chocolate, Corning dinner sets, Sanyo rice cookers, Braun grinders-mixers, Sony Walkmans, Seiko watches, blue jeans, Johnny Walker, Chivas Regal, Ray-Bans, two-in-ones, VCRs; nothing was too small, everything had its own little aura and each and everyone

131

got something. Each fragment spoke to the broader mosaic of a world of IPE, the portrait of a world as it should be, could be and was, just across the border.

Three weeks of vacation go by pretty quickly but three weeks every year could work up a lot of enthusiasm in a school kid for jumping across the divide. So for the rest of the year you went back, or were sent back, to your books, to studying for your competitive exams. Everyone knew that acing your exams was the only way to jump from Development into IPE. And everyone knew that IPE was where one would be richer, whiter and lighter in mien.

There was nothing to really argue about here.

Appearances were reality.

Fiction was fact.

What was visible was a clear border that needed to be crossed. What never crossed my mind was any sense of a consciousness that was somehow false or in anyway unreal.

III

My Thin Skin, Their Red-White Theory

I am teaching POLI 268, "The Politics of Globalization."

We are reading Thomas Friedman's *The World is Flat*.[2] That has been the first book students read in this class for a while. It was *The Lexus and Olive Tree* before.[3] Other texts have come and gone. But Friedman—in one form or another—has remained steady on my list of required reading. Why do I prescribe him, my colleagues wonder? Others kid me that I am only making an obnoxious writer unnecessarily richer.

I offer a variety of reasons, some hermeneutic, some tactical, some served up on the spur of the moment: It's the dominant ideology, the way many influential Americans understand globalization. It's the book the students in my classes are most likely to encounter at home, in conversations with their parents and it's important for me to begin where they begin. Unlike many of you, I plead, I don't subscribe to the *New York Times*; so I feel a little less implicated by the prospect of making the truly obnoxious richer.

Real reasons or not, that's what I offer.

Friedman, as you know, is glowing in his account of globalization, of the "flattening of the world." He is particularly appreciative of what's happening in China, India and in places like Beijing, Shanghai, Bangalore and Hyderabad.

I recall one interview of Friedman's with Rajesh Rao, founder and CEO of a games company.[4] Friedman presents him as an embodiment of what he calls the "triple convergence" and a good example of "what happens when an Indian zippie plugs into the ten flatteners." After a great deal of explaining and praise of what Rao's company is up to, Friedman notes his "raw ambition" and what that might imply for Americans. And Rajesh's words echo a mutual respect and admiration for the ambitious nature of his imagined Americans:

> People like me have learned a lot from Americans. We have learned to become a little more aggressive in the way we market ourselves... What is really necessary is for everybody to wake up to the fact that there is a fundamental shift that is happening in the way people are going to do business. And everyone is going to have to improve themselves and be able to compete. ...If you are seeing all this energy coming out of Indians, it's because we have been underdogs and we have that drive to kind of achieve and to get there...India is going to be a superpower and we are going to rule.

In response to Friedman's question about whom India will rule, Rajesh laughs and clarifies "his choice of words":

It's not about ruling anybody. That's the point. There is nobody to rule anymore. It's about how you can create opportunities where you can thrive. I think today that rule is about efficiency, it's about collaboration and it is about competitiveness and it is about being a player. It is about staying sharp and being in the game…The world is a football field now and you've got to be sharp to be on the team which plays on that field. If you're not good enough, you're going to be sitting and watching the game. That's all.

I wonder, sometimes, if I teach Friedman because I am, like the Rajesh Raos of Friedman's world, powerfully taken up, narrated into an I, by the thrill of fictions like the one above. What grabs me here is Rajesh's framing of his story in terms of a movement from underdog to global player. I see myself read in those fictions: the fundamental shift from colonized, powerless underdogs to Third World nationalism, from endless deliberations of North-South, New International Economic Order, Preferences for the Third World, Darfur to Global Economy, Davos, Doha, G-8 invitations, Sovereign Wealth Funds, Overflowing Foreign Exchange Reserves, Lenovo etc. I suspect I read the same desire in millions of other Chinese and Indians and Vietnamese and Puerto Ricans and Malaysians and Indonesians and Koreans and Iranians and others struggling, if only imaginatively, to liberate themselves from the burden of belonging to or being a species from and of Development.

Players, at last! Don't I like the feeling that those in his books—those in Development—no longer appear as pathetic Third World victims, but as threats to be taken seriously, threats to the smugness and arrogance of the status quo and of those in IPE? Isn't it a relief to see at least some of the ex-colonized as "players," as states, places, peoples and names that can no longer be ignored, as fellow human beings competing with you, chasing you to the top rather than a species waiting to be helped in one way or another?

Wasn't that the burden of our post-coloniality and the very condition of our entry into modernity? Haven't I, and millions of these other species from Development learnt, painfully and in a hundred different ways, that IPE, to follow the claims of Blaney and Inayatullah here, is "a culture of competition"? Don't we know, even if we don't always explicitly remember it or acknowledge it, that our prominent choices in IPE, or even within the narrower political economy of graduate school and the academic field of IR, are either to be "players" or risk being objects/spectators/failures, risk being exterminated? Isn't the learning of those "English lessons"[5] primarily what explains my and their presence here among you today rather than a hundred others—better human beings in so many ways—that I can name? Isn't that the secret of our success in crossing the colonial divide between Development and IPE and in even being heard on these issues?

But then, am I not also a little embarrassed to be confessing this? As if, somehow, I am lacking the right scholarly or radical credentials? Not scholarly enough to be American IPE and not radical enough to be British IPE?[6] A double deficiency? Aren't/shouldn't people like me be deported back to Development?

Why the sense, however fleeting, of a double lack in confessing this? Is it because in acknowledging this, I also recognize the superficiality, the moral thinness of what is being admitted to? If I relate very meaningfully to the ambitions of colonized underdogs to be finally human, even if only as players in a highly competitive game, why do I also feel obliged to frame it as something less than fulfilling on multiple counts?

Am I convinced that IPE somehow is not a study of global players and super-powers and how they rule, how they govern those less than super? Do those who study IPE study anything else, anything morally thicker? And if they don't, are they even remotely embarrassed by that knowledge? Do they feel any lack in how they are narrated by their fictions, fictions that are meaningful to them and constitutive of them? Or, is there, always already, only an excess there, an excess of the real, the rigorous and the radical?

IV

Desires, Global and Local

In writing this paper, I felt, in typical postcolonial fashion, an intense need to "catch up" with the latest work in IPE. So, over spring break, I scoured the journals and books at the Wilson Library of the University of Minnesota. But the more I traversed the field of contemporary IPE, the more I found myself outside its borders. I just couldn't see myself playing this game anymore. It seemed so lacking in life, so, for want of an academic enough term, boring; it had a certain sort of rigor but not much life—rigor mortis, you could say.

Naming names, let us dwell, for a moment, on the recent review of the field of IPE in RIPE by Benjamin Cohen.[7] Based on his *International Political Economy: An Intellectual History*,[8] it distinguishes the field of IPE into two spaces, one of an American IPE and the other, a British IPE. The argument is nuanced in terms of the distinctions it makes between American and British IPEs. The distinction allocates positivism, empiricism, methodological rigor, objectivity and narrowness to one side and a more historical focus, multi-disciplinarity, insightfulness and maybe less rigor but a seemingly greater concern for normative issues to the other side. One side stars Keohane, Nye, Krasner, Katzenstein and Gilpin; the other side stars Strange and Cox. There is a debate on this division. Higgott and Watson[9] object on grounds that Cohen's division is structured implicitly in favor of and on the terms of American IPE. Ravenhill[10] talks about an excluded middle and they all make points that are, I am willing to grant, probably correct in terms of a certain bounding of this field.

But why am I not moved intellectually or emotionally by that imagination? What is wrong with me, I wonder, that a state of the art review of the field by its foremost thinker and a debate around it by other scholars renowned in the field does little to excite me, doesn't pull me in, doesn't captivate me but only induces, at best, a sense of scholarly duty—a sense that I should note these articles for citation and for their easy ability to categorize a complex world but that nothing there will induce any intellectual growth or understanding within me or my students? That, in many ways, we might be better off meandering aimlessly with Friedman—a Friedman over a Cohen? Heresy, you might say. What underdeveloped thinking, what poverty of theory here!

Maybe, I am prepared to confess, what this illustrates, more than anything else, is my provinciality in terms of IPE. Maybe I have progressively "de-skilled" myself to a point where I am just not ready to be a diligent scholar of this field. Maybe I lack the will, the rigor, the objectivity, the technical skills and the diligence that are probably required to keep abreast of the deathly developments in this field. But while I am open and willing to hear those limitations, I also want to explore what appears to me to be the problem here.

So once more, to the superficial.

First of all, if IPE is a game, a local quarrel and reconciliation between American and British cousins, however generously defined, what does it have to do with the rest of us, a global majority, in the world? Is bridging a "transatlantic divide" (over a self-admitted "pond") or debating the presence/absence of a divide over that pond, its excluded middle etc. or the prominently heroic Uncles or charmingly crazy Aunts—the stars of this game—who write, live and die on its shores, sufficient to produce a space meaningfully large and valid enough to be called the "international," to address the global?

Second, could we argue that others, all of us locals in so many ways, should pay attention to IPE because its scholars grasp realities that are, in many ways, more than or somehow extend beyond their local selves? Could we argue that the American IPE scholars, who pride themselves so much on their objectivity and rigor, are in any way really global in that sense?

Here is Cohen's presentation of that case:

> Globally, the dominant version of IPE (we might even say the hegemonic version) is one that has developed in the US, where most scholarship tends to hew close to the norms of conventional social science. In the "American school," priority is given to scientific method—what might be called a pure science or hard science model. Analysis is based on the twin principles of positivism and empiricism, which hold that knowledge is best accumulated through an appeal to objective observation and systematic testing. In the words of Stephen Krasner, one of the American school's leading lights: "International Political Economy is deeply embedded in the standard methodology of the social sciences which, stripped to its bare bones, simply means stating a proposition and testing it against external evidence." Even its critics concede that the mainstream American version of IPE may be regarded as the prevailing orthodoxy.[11]

If hegemony is coercion plus consent, then consent is what is not easily coming from within me to this formulation of American IPE as an orthodoxy with any explanatory power. Why this obtuseness on my part?

I offer one excuse, and it is only an excuse.

Glancing through the issues of the same journal, I chanced across another article by a prominent scholar of decolonization, Jan Nederveen Pieterse. Writing about what he calls "political and economic brinksmanship," Pieterse recounts an exchange with Joseph Nye, one of the pioneers of American IPE:

> At a recent meeting of the American Political Science Association, Joseph Nye said "the United States cannot win by hard power alone, but must pay more heed to soft power and global communications." I asked him why should the United States win and he replied, "the United States must win because it is the world's largest democracy and this is a dangerous world."[12]

I wish to quibble not with Pieterse but with Nye. The United States is referred to often as the world's most powerful democracy, not as its largest, because it is not the largest. But even if that were so how do we relate to a perspective that takes it for granted that some aspect of the self, the local space in which one belongs, or sees oneself as belonging to, must win, must prevail over others and yet is venerated, by the field, as "objective"?

I see the similarities here between Nye, Rajesh Rao and myself: India or China or the Third World must rule. Become superpowers, because they were underdogs. The US, Europe, the West, must win—because they are democracies in a dangerous world. But there is a difference. My claim of Third World nationalism around the thrill of finally competing with the global players also induces in me not only a sense of embarrassment, but is likely to be read as the sign of a double lack: insufficiently rigorous, insufficiently radical. I am a little embarrassed and uneasy with my desire and my implication in this competitive self. And I cannot claim any objectivity in my defense or even an easy disengagement from superficial provincialities in favor of a global radicalism.

I wonder if Joseph Nye is embarrassed in any way by his provincial desires. Or Krasner or Katzenstein or Cohen or Gilpin? Are they embarrassed when their principles and their affiliations, the knowledge they generate and the interests that are served seem to overlap so neatly? Or, do they believe they are only being objective because they have stumbled onto the universal unlike us provincials?

Moreover, what of the radicals? Some of my students and many of my friends, including many from India itself, are always outraged by stories such as those of Rajesh Rao and their desires to be global players. My radical friends and students talk about capitalism, about consumerism, about exploitation. Their criticisms of stories such as these come quick and fast. I can't help but wonder if they have heard all this before. How does the superficiality of this superficial way of being in the world come so easily for them while I struggle through my provincial embeddedness for it? How morally thin am I really? How deeply embedded in an underdog's development/under-development imaginary? How not so universal—either on a liberal front or a radical one?

Maybe I am being unfair but the feeling that these are easy criticisms for the radicals to make nags me. I find myself hesitating to quickly criticize Friedman's superficiality and thinness and move on though I have already structured the class texts in that fashion. The students will soon be reading Stiglitz, Anna Tsing, Timothy Mitchell, Hardt and Negri. But I want them to soak in Friedman, to understand the meaningfulness, the lived-depth of that thinness. Is this because I suspect, maybe unjustly, that their deep critiques of capitalism are also masks, appearances, differently designed, but thin and superficial in their own way?

Am I pitting my magical desires, desires for magic, against theirs?

Why?

Is there anything meaningful at stake here other than an insufficiently critical ego, anything other than the historical misfortune, the contingency, of crossing the border into IPE from the other side of the tracks, from Development?

Am I willing and able to cross the colonial divide only materially but not ethically? Why/what am I holding back?

V

The New Colonialists, Iraq and the Multiple Logics of Violence

A recent issue of *The Economist* is titled "The New Colonialists." On the cover it shows some khaki-clad, pith-helmeted people, among others, trekking across a desert on camels. Intrigued I flicked through its web pages to see what the story was about: the US? Iraq? Not really. I should have known. It was about China and its apparently prodigious appetite for resources (pork among others) and the potential upside and downside to that. What was the term colonialist doing there, I couldn't help wondering? How easy, how careless and how violent a gesture? A centuries old history of colonialism is turned around ever so casually to brand precisely those who had barely emerged from colonialism; whose counter-violence, even if it was in any way similar to that of the old colonialists, is barely three decades old.

I see such facile gestures all around me. China on Darfur appears to overwrite the US in Iraq.[13] Iran in Iraq or Iran on nuclear reactors is supposed to blind me to the strangeness of the US in Iraq or the US on its new generation of nuclear and space weaponry. The EU on Turkey's human rights shouts down the fate of Turks in Germany and of Muslims in France, Britain and Denmark. North Africans on the Southern shores of Europe and Albanians in Italy are assumed to wash out the continuity of colonial Spanish enclaves and French, Belgian and British colonial influences in Africa. And so on.

Are these merely careless gestures? Or is the carelessness also a sign and result of unequal power; of how easily some of us can cross over to/cross out the other side and come back without really having to worry about being stopped, challenged or questioned?

Colonial Cares

An indignant article in a 2008 issue of *The Washington Post*[14] notes how German police, using a "little-known Nazi-era law," are prosecuting Americans using titles such as Doctor when these have not been granted by German Universities. Not surprisingly, a number of those affected found the law "absurd, totally absurd." The reporters explain the issue by drawing our attention to the "formal" and hierarchical nature of Germany and the resulting "social demotion" involved in "forcing Americans to forsake their titles:"

> The proper use of honorifics is no small matter in Germany, a society given to formality where even longtime neighbors insist on addressing each other using their surnames. Those with advanced degrees like to show them off, and it is not uncommon to earn more than one. A male faculty member with two PhDs can fully expect to be called "Herr Professor Dr. Dr. Schmidt," for example. In effect, forcing Americans to forsake their titles amounts to a social demotion. "It's an indication of the hierarchization of German society," said Gary Smith, director of the American Academy in Berlin. "Germans are much more status-conscious about these things, and the status is real."[15]

What is directly relevant to our purposes here is the claim about the absurdity of the whole situation. As Gary Smith points out, "It's really an absurd situation in a globalized world." For some strange reason, this reminds me of the debates in IPE. Is it because what it obsesses about as absurd makes invisible injustices far more significant than the inability of Americans to be called Doktor?

I am not claiming that what the article points out, the "social demotion" of Americans with titles in Germany, is necessarily untrue. But is that what's really absurd here, or in "a globalized world"? Don't we know already that nation-states, particularly those in IPE, routinely devalorize and demote the social and economic and cultural values of others? That in the US itself, hundreds of thousands of human beings with advanced skills, degrees and credentials from other places are structurally demoted in terms of their economic skills and forced to make a living as taxi-drivers or newspaper vendors or grocery baggers or cooks in restaurants only because their crossing across the colonial divide from Development into IPE has not been certified by authorities in IPE? Don't we know that, for many of us from Development, our very condition of entry into the space of IPE is graded and graduated precisely, every step of the way, in terms of formal and correct educational qualifications (how many immigration points is a B.A. or a Ph.D. in Canada or Australia?), high skills (H-1B), rare skills, being "outstanding," being a "genius" (easy Green Cards)?

Our bodies and brains are weighed, measured, graded, our character assessed for its worthiness and its integrity before we are even allowed to enter provisionally, in order to do jobs that people in IPE cannot now do. Our stay in IPE is conditional on demand and supply for our "gradably" high skills, our continuing competitiveness and, nowadays, even an assessment of our insecurity-terrorist potential. Our families can get deported or sent back from the airport itself or not even allowed in if, in some minor functionary's view, the paper trail does not attest to a transparent and good life certified by and attested to by various authorities.

For those of us from Development who crossed over to IPE without waiting respectfully in line because we couldn't wait hungrily any more, don't we now wait in market-places early in the morning—waiting, hoping to be picked up by one contractor or another? Isn't every day a lottery, a game of chance played with the muscles and the stomach at stake? Isn't every gaze that is accidentally met by us an invitation to be scanned more thoroughly and inspected and detained or deported? We know all this. We've known this for a while now. We know about those who are forced to be hidden in the shadows and those who are forced to be transparently lily-white in the limelight (our pictures and finger-prints were data-based long before 9/11).

And yet, our worlds are rarely visible in meaningful ways from IPE. They appear only to the extent that we threaten to compete, and the nation-states that we come from threaten to gobble up resources that are assumed to suddenly be "common" and "global,"[16] or jobs that are suddenly designated as "private" and "national."

What is presented as absurd for a globalized economy though, in terms of that article and the slew of reports that played that up, is the denial of equality—a Nazi-era law (hint, hint)—within the space of IPE to those of the West. But do such anxieties, such petty battles across little ponds, even begin to get at the visible and invisible divides that separate IPE from Development?

I am afraid this is still partly about those in Development who can make a living, who can try to produce and maybe sporadically consume. This is still about those who are defined by their engagement with the spaces of production in IPE. Shouldn't we also talk, maybe mourn, those who are being destroyed *en masse*, because these spaces of production have decided to cross over into their lives, to rid them of weapons of mass destruction, to develop them into democracies, to help rescue their women and children and other such benighted animals?[17] We know that even if we don't admit to counting their numbers officially, we do value them, just not at the same rates as we value ourselves.[18] We do care.

Yes. We care. But why? Or, how do we understand the inequality of care? In other words, why is humanitarianism, like so much else in IR/IPE, also a gesture from IPE to Development, from the white and rich to the poor and non-white?

Adam Hochschild, in narrating the atrocities in the Congo under Belgian colonization, mentions a seemingly trivial incident to highlight the less savory aspects of Henry Morton Stanley.[19] He points out that at one point in his expedition across Africa, Stanley cut the tail of his dog, cooked it and fed it to him. I find, in teaching Hochschild, that this small incident arouses as much, if not greater disgust, among the students in International Politics as the account of eight million dead or the pictures and individual stories remembered in the book. I have always wondered why.

There seems to be some fundamental violation here even though it is possible to argue that the tails of dogs are cut routinely for cosmetic reasons. Is it the pain inflicted on an "innocent" and helpless animal? Is it some sense that the integrity of the relationship between human and pet is being violated? Is it the lack of any obviously meaningful reason for this action? A number of likely reasons are offered when we discuss what it is about this incident that they find disturbing. Why does this incident rise so clearly to the top of one's consciousness when there are pictures of adults and children whose hands have been cut, women who have been held hostage, assaulted, men whipped, killed and brutalized in a variety of ways? What is it about a puppy being fed its tail that gives it equal if not greater status in the imagination as that of the deaths of millions of Congolese?

I don't really know, though I have my suspicions. But this equality/inequality in status between puppies and other beings came to the fore more recently in the furor over a recent video on YouTube. A Marine's family in the US has been receiving death threats and has been at the center of a storm of public protest over a video that was shot and posted over YouTube.[20] That video, the authenticity of which has not been verified, allegedly shows this Marine tossing a puppy over a cliff. One of the more intrepid freshmen in the class first brought this to my attention in an email. He had also, it turned out, done some additional "research" on this story:

Mr. Muppidi,

A story of a soldier who threw a puppy off a cliff in Iraq is swamping the internet. I looked into where the incident occurred and found out it was in Haditha. I remembered something about Haditha. What I remembered was the Haditha murders where 24 civilians were executed by a soldier. I was curious to see how the interest of each story compared so I looked on Google Trends. I'm still working on the numbers but it appears the puppy's death is attracting more attention. However, both are dwarfed by the outing of an American idol contestant as a gay stripper.

God help us,

[A. Student]

This student's email clearly raises a number of issues worth thinking through, not the least of which is the question of which issues raise our outrage and which ones don't. But, clearly, what is not missing publicly is outrage. Am I upset about a puppy being thrown over a cliff? Yes, of course. But can I be outraged enough about it or outraged enough about Stanley feeding his dog its tail—outraged enough to issue death threats, write protest letters, do something—without that outrage in some way testifying to the politics of my perspective and what it both highlights and blinds me to? If you insist, however, on limiting your interest in my answer to the question of the puppy alone (Are you against the throwing of puppies over cliffs? Yes or No?) or if, in your more radical moments, you are willing to see how some of us on the Development side are also puppy killers and you want to know all the concrete details because the meta-narrative is already known to you and you are sympathetic to it and insist on sharing your solidarity, then how do we even begin to have a conversation? If you insist on reading anything other than a fully-fledged, repeated and sustained engagement in this practice as testifying to all sorts of technical and humanitarian and radical lacunae within me, then how do I get to discuss, make visible or even focus on all that is being drowned out by this rigor and/or radicalism of yours? When do other Hadithas, other teleologies, other meta-narratives, other humanities, other economies become visible to you? How do they cross the colonial divide to enter into the imagination of IPE if those in Development are constantly forced to talk and take stances in terms primarily of puppies being thrown over cliffs?

I suspect that, at the end of the day, Stanley fed his dog its tail because, among a number of other things, he could. The soldier threw the puppy over the cliff because, among a number of things, he could. We keep animals in zoos and lock others into Development because we care for them and love them, and want to protect them, and see them and observe them and learn about them but also, because we can. And because they can't really refuse; because, whatever their desires, they are not really in a position to say no to our desire to see them and love them and care for them and know them and protect them. And so, IPE talks endlessly about itself and its superficialities, because it can. Yes, it can; yes, they can. And it is very important, in their deepest moments of self-doubt to have that desire affirmed. Yes, they can. Isn't the corollary of that, though, for those at the receiving end: Yes, we can, but no, you can't. Not you. Not yet. Not now. Maybe never. And, however superficial and thin it may seem, saying no to that negation ends up being a meaningful first step, an ethical step, a humanizing step, for those in Development trying to cross the colonial divide. It cannot remain there. It might end up moving elsewhere. But I do understand that step, maybe more so than some others.

And that's why, as you seek to rush through that moment, to seek salvation elsewhere, in rigor or radicalism, I want to delay your journey a bit.

I want to request you to wait, listen and seek to make sense of some of those superficialities, those thin-nesses, those masks and those ideologies.

7

COGNITION AND COMPLICITY

Some Worlds that Came Ashore in Louisiana

Hurricane Katrina hit the coast of New Orleans in the last week of August 2005. Foreseen as one of the three worst possible crises likely to hit the US, the Bush administration's response to it was less than stellar. Much has been written on that and it is not my intention to rehash those criticisms here. I am drawn more to some of the other issues that came ashore with Hurricane Katrina. These were somewhat brief glimpses, unexpected visibilities, of other worlds, other ways of being, as they were conjured from within the borders of the United States. I wish to begin this chapter by drawing attention to two terms—"third world," and "refugee"—that were deployed over and over again in political criticism and public commentary in the aftermath of Katrina.

Writing in the *New York Times*, Maureen Dowd ("United States of Shame"?) wondered: "Who are we if we can't take care of our own?" The answer to that question, it appeared, resided not within the US but outside of itself, in the international realm and in a specific imagination of that realm. The explicit question here was whether the United States, in failing to respond adequately to Hurricane Katrina, had shown itself to be not the United States ("Who are we...") but some other entity, something that, unlike the US, could not "take care of [its] own." But who were these others? Who are those who can be thought of, fairly common-sensically, as not taking care of their own? Those nominated included cities, countries and continents: "Baghdad,"[1] "Bangladesh," "Somalia," "Rwanda," and Africa.

The devastation in New Orleans, in many ways, was a domestic issue. Unlike 9/11, it had little to do with the obvious actions of other actors or states in the world. Why then were these cities, countries or continents from outside the US and North America being invoked? What did Bangladesh, Rwanda, Somalia or Ethiopia have to do with New Orleans? On what understanding of the international realm, of their own world and that of others, were these evocations grounded?

The Subject of Sovereignty

> Debbie Brooks has never been to Ethiopia, but after two intermi-
> nable days spent atop a stretch of Interstate 10 here, she now
> knows what it means to be starving under a baking sun, watch-
> ing family members deteriorate by the hour. "I have lived that
> experience now," she said Friday afternoon from the patch of
> concrete she, her father and aunt have called home since dawn
> Thursday. "This is like the Third World."[2]

Two days of starvation under a hot sun on Interstate 10 can, no doubt, be seen as a harsh experience. But how is it that this experience, which can be linked to multiple other traumatic experiences (for instance, the experience of being stranded on Interstates in adverse weather conditions), is readily translated into a particular knowledge of Ethiopia and the Third World, of international relations? How does this act to produce knowledge of ("she now knows") places outside the US, especially one that has never been visited ("has never been to Ethiopia") or another world altogether ("like the Third World")? What is the source of Debbie Brooks's certainty of global geography and relations?

Katrina also brought home another issue: what to call the people displaced by it? While newscasters initially relied on calling them "refugees," the NAACP and political leaders such as the Rev. Jesse Jackson objected to the term, saying that it was an example of "racist language:"[3] Following Jackson's objection, there was much discussion about what exactly were the "images provoked" by the term "refugee." Kelly Crossley, a media critic, noted the images that came to her: "If you think about a refugee, what comes to mind are those people walking across borders in the Sudan, walking across Somalia. And in your head, you see those people as persons of color without a home, carrying everything they own in one bag."

I have already raised the question of why is it that these are the equivalencies that are established. I want to raise the additional question of the negative charge to the images: Even if these images were unproblematic, what exactly is it that is negative about them in the mind of the person making the connections? One can very well picture people walking across borders in the Sudan or Somalia. One can agree that maybe they are persons of color without a home and carrying everything they own in one bag. But so what? What is it that is "negative" about finding oneself in a condition without too many possessions or absent a home? What is the unstated charge at work here?

It needs to be noted, before proceeding further, that some people did raise objections to such negative associations. The President of Refugees International, an advocacy organization, protested against the association of "refugee" with "negative" connotations or with any racial profiling:

There are thousands and thousands of refugees in the United States, hundreds of thousands. And they don't fit any sort of racial pattern. These are people who are fleeing for their lives, fleeing for freedom, trying to find a better life for themselves and their children. That's what the term "refugee" means to me. And many of these people have great dignity and have that dignity in the face of great loss and trauma.[4]

Could we argue, then, taking such objections seriously, that the problem is not necessarily that these are people of color or without many possessions or a home but that of an assumed/ likely "loss" of dignity under these conditions? But if dignity is a sensibility of "pride and self-respect" or of "worthiness" or a "condition of being worthy of respect, esteem or honor,"[5] should we assume, necessarily, that not having a home or having only a few possessions or suffering "great loss and trauma" are destructive of one's "pride and self-respect" or sense of "worthiness"? Within what social imaginary, what understanding of the international, would such a translation or association not only make sense but be seen as necessary?

It also emerges, though, that the problem may not be just the Other's presumed loss of dignity but also the threat of losing one's own dignity when burdened with the presence of this wretched Other. Bob Garfield of NPR put it this way:

...[R]efugees, however dignified they may be, tend eventually to represent a burden to those who take them in, a drain on resources and ever present reminder of misery. Like the crippled and the scarred and the urban homeless, they make us uncomfortable. Dehumanization is but one step away.[6]

What the mark of "refugee" does then is not just to establish equivalences to other personal qualities—dignity, self-respect or worthiness—but also to require a certain relationship to the refugee Other from the non-refugee Self. In nominating you as a refugee I am demanding a certain orientation of myself towards you. That obligation, within this imaginary, comes primarily as a feeling of "discomfort," in the form of unsettling the self and making it "uncomfortable." Hence the equivalence between refugees and those who are "crippled … scarred and … homeless." These are those subjects of international relations who do not fit the accepted definitions of entities in that they lack some essential features necessary for that fullness. They are, in many ways (corporeally, aesthetically, psychologically, materially) crucially incomplete and hence not fully sovereign. Maybe we can read them as the human equivalent of "failed" states. Failed humans live in failed states. Refugees live in the Third World. You can have dignity in the face of failure. But you cannot have completeness or fullness. That is the privilege of the sovereign.

The Spaces of Sovereignty

That this was also the imaginary within which Rev. Jackson was articulating his concern is evident in his speech:

> The media says, "Well, these are refugees." No, no, no. These are citizens—not refugees but citizens, American citizens. (Applause and cheers). We are not refugees. We are citizens. (Applause). We protect refugees because we care. The sign on the Statue of Liberty says, "Give me your tired, your poor, your huddled masses who yearn to breathe free." These are refugees we're reaching out to who are escaping some form of political persecution or famine or starvation. We receive refugees and then they become citizens. Refugees exist on privilege. Citizens exist on rights. We have a right to be protected. We are lucky. We are Americans. (Applause and cheers).[7]

Jackson's narrative makes a distinction between US citizens and foreign refugees and also between an American inside and a foreign outside. US citizenship represents an identity of fullness, which is, partly, a question of luck but also of certain rights, among which are the "right to be protected," to be taken care of by our own, as a matter of right. Between citizens and refugees there is an asymmetric relationship deriving from the asymmetry of their "places of origin." US citizenship is a question of rights whereas refugee-hood is a transitional state on the way to citizenship. Citizens care for refugees but being a refugee is a special right bestowed by citizens on those coming in from the outside. Refugees come from an outside where they were tired, poor or yearning to be free. The outside is an incomplete space, a place of political persecution, famine or starvation. That refugees are coming to the US from the outside means that similar negative conditions do not or cannot exist on the inside, within the US. Such existence would be incompatible with one's understanding of what the US was.

While Jackson's presentation of the US is interesting in a number of ways, what I'll focus on here is the need for its reiteration in the context of Hurricane Katrina. Why, one could ask, in the context of a domestic issue, was Jackson so anxious to assert a difference, an asymmetry—an asymmetry between sovereign citizens and dependent refugees—that is predicated on an asymmetry between global spaces, between the US and other countries?

I would argue that this is where the images that come to Kelly Crossley's mind become relevant. For Crossley, people of color walking with very few possessions and without a home across Sudan or Somalia represent troubling associations with the term refugee. Implicit in that understanding is an expectation of a completed identity, of fullness, of US citizenship. In this state of fullness, dignity is directly connected to material abundance: to having possessions, a home, and of rarely having to walk across long distances in a seemingly vulnerable condition. What this expectation makes invisible is the fact that vast numbers of US citizens do not necessarily have access to citizenship in this "fuller" sense (though they might have it as a condition to be achieved). Their sudden emergence, their abrupt visibility, then becomes a stark and uncomfortable reminder of the incomplete nature of the space inside, of the lacks, of the misery that still exists and the burdens on the sovereign subjects, the citizens, which could follow.

Hurricane Katrina made visible a world of US citizens who were already internal refugees in terms of the dominant imaginary. The fact that many were also people of color was especially disturbing since that combination is constitutive of the dominant understanding of the places outside. Within such an imaginary, for a citizen to be classified as a refugee is to automatically suffer some losses. Their demands would appear not as demands for their rights but as a burden on sovereign subjects. They cannot but be constantly produced in an unequal relationship as they appear, visually and otherwise, before full-fledged citizens. It is the production of this unequal/asymmetrical relationship that the Reverend can be seen as trying to forestall by calling such a deployment "racist." In not calling the domestic victims of Katrina refugees, it is the power to nominate themselves that was partially conceded.

As Kelly Crossley observed:

> I've heard a lot of people saying that we're playing word games at a time of crisis. This is ridiculous. But you know what? Basically, that sentiment came from people who have not been on the other end of language directed at them in a negative way that had the power to hurt. So when you have been at the other end of that and you know what that feels like and you know what the impact of that is over days, over weeks, over years, over centuries, then this is really quite important. It's not a word game. It's really not a politically correct thing. It really has to do with paying attention to people's humanity.[8]

This focus on "paying attention to people's humanity" inside the US is surely laudable. But it is also worth asking if this can be achieved only by bartering away, in that process, the humanities of many others inhabiting spaces outside the US? Who, one might ask, was paying attention to the "humanity" of those who lived in Bangladesh, Somalia, Ethiopia, Rwanda and Baghdad?

II

Europe and Africa Meet in Virginia

Campaigning in southwest Virginia, on 11 August 2006, George Allen, the Republican Senator from Virginia, also a potential US Presidential candidate for 2008, began his speech by indicating his desire to "run this campaign on positive, constructive ideas."[9] But the positivity he sought to produce began, fairly quickly, to run out of control as he welcomed a volunteer for his opponent, by referring to him as a "macaca": "This fellow here, over here with the yellow shirt, macaca, or whatever his name is. He's with my opponent. He's following us around everywhere. And it's just great."[10] Warming to his theme, Allen said, "Let's give a welcome to macaca, here. Welcome to America and the real world of Virginia."[11] As it turned out though, it was Allen that suddenly found himself welcomed into worlds, worlds constituted and haunted by colonialisms that he probably had little intention or desire to reawaken at that moment.

The "macaca" Allen was referring to and welcoming into the "real world of Virginia," had some claims on being a "real" Virginian himself (when it emerged subsequently that he, unlike Senator Allen, had been born in that state). S.R. Sidharth was twenty years old, an American citizen and a fourth year student of the University of Virginia. He was also the only person of color at the rally. The controversy, in the media, over Allen's remarks swirled primarily around his intentions in using that term, what it meant, and whether the Senator was being "racist" or not. Allen's campaign tried to shape the emerging archive on this issue by claiming that Allen was actually picking up a nickname that his campaign staff had adopted for Sidharth (based on his hairstyle) and that the comments had little or nothing to do with his skin color or his seeming outsider-ness in that context. While Allen's intentions are important in some ways, what is more crucial for our purposes here, are the worlds that he unwittingly bumbled into in southwest Virginia and resurrected nationally.

As the controversy spread, the Wikipedia community,[12] among others, dug into the historical and zoological archives to excavate the international connections that might have gone into the production and circulation of this specific form of address: it turned out that "macaca" was a derivation from the "name of the genus comprised of the macaque primates" and was a "dismissive epithet used by Francophone colonials in Africa for native populations of North and Sub-saharan Africans." It noted that "in the Belgian Congo, colonial whites continued to call Africans *macaques* and insist that they had only recently come down from trees"; that the "word is still occasionally used in Belgium (both in Flanders and Wallonia) as a racial slur, referring not to Congolese but to Moroccan immigrants or their descendants;" that "In the Adventures of Tintin written by Belgian writer-artist Hergé, Captain Haddock uses the term *macaque* as an insult, along with other terms with racial overtones." It also emerged that the Senator's mother was "a French colonial born in Tunisia who emigrated to the United States following World War II."[13] The usage that I found most fascinating in the entire line-up that came to light was that of Patrice Lumumba. It turns out that, in 1960, at a ceremony at which Belgium gave the Congo its independence, Prime Minister Lumumba gave a "speech accusing Belgian King Baudouin of presiding over a "regime of injustice, suppression, and exploitation" before ending [by saying] "We are no longer your *macaques*," as the Congolese in the audience rose to their feet cheering."[14]

In August 2006, in southwest Virginia, a Senator's words evoked specters beyond anything he could have foreseen or controlled. They threatened to bury an ambitious political career. Is this an issue best understood as a question of ignorance or racism? Or, as one more sign of the multiple and wondrous worlds that embrace, constitute and collide on a mundane basis in our daily encounters with each other?

III

The Grilling Fields of Iraq

Abeer Qassim Hamza al-Janabi was fourteen years old when four soldiers of the US army in Iraq "killed her mother, father, five-year-old sister," raped her, "murdered her, drenched the bodies with kerosene, and set them on fire."[15] I am supposed to put "allegedly" here somewhere or add "according to a statement by one of the accused," in the earlier sentence but can't quite get myself to do it. I do want to add the sentence that follows in the report: "Then the GIs grilled chicken wings."[16]

Robin Morgan, the author of the article from which I have quoted, in writing about this incident and the subsequent trial of the GIs, argues that the "US military is now a mercenary force," that it has a "poverty draft," and that, as feminist scholars have been arguing for a while, military training involves the systematic eroticization of violence: "How can," she asks, "rape not be central to the propaganda that violence is erotic—a pervasive message affecting everything from US foreign policy to 'camouflage chic' and glamorized gangsta styles?"[17]

"Violence is erotic." What does that mean? How is that "message/meaning" articulated, made meaningful, circulated, received? Violence has to do, in one sense, with the application of force on, a violation of, a wronging of another. Eroticism is about passion, love, desire for and with another. What must be added to violence such that the imposition of oneself on another, the disregard of her will, desires and passions, the degradation of her body, can actually be read/seen as equivalent to ("is") eroticism? In this equation, violence can be erotic only if the difference that I make, can make, will make, the passions that are inflamed in me by your actions, are irrelevant to the satisfaction of your urges, your needs. Subtract me from the overall equation. Then "eroticism" is about your desire for me, but not with me. When I am in, when I am held, forced, beheld, I remain but only a material substrate and not a being whose feelings, senses, perspectives, desires, or wills need to be deferred to. Think chicken wings.

Let us try again. The key to spreading the message may not be that violence is erotic but maybe that violence is pleasurable. Violence, the violation of another, the overcoming of another against their will, the ravaging of another against their resistance to your desire, is an activity that need not arouse disgust or self-loathing but can actually generate positive, pleasurable, emotions in the self. These chicken wings taste very good. How did you grill them? In that context, it is absurd to ask about the worldviews, the feelings, the well-being, the needs and pleasures of the chicken (except to the extent that they may affect the overall taste) for us.

Violence is pleasurable under conditions where the other is always already constituted as chicken, as meat, as a body (biological, zoological, social, national), a material substrate to be worked over (chopped, marinated, smoked, grilled), reworked (developed, transformed, modernized, intervened) to produce something that looks, tastes and feels good and correct to us. Violence is pleasurable primarily under colonial conditions, within social relationships that are structured on the discriminatory inclusion of the other, relationships that include the bodies of the other but exclude their voices and worldviews. We have vehement debates over how to rework the chicken, what spices to mix, what sauces to pour, how to grill but never stop, cannot stop, to ask the chicken.

We can, following Morgan, surely recognize the "eroticization of violence" in military training in the US and elsewhere. But we also need to recognize the systematic presence of a colonial imaginary here—one that is productive of the "eroticization" (as self-pleasure) of violence through the construction and sustenance of a specific sort of world politics, a world in which the bodies of others (biological, zoological, social, national) are included but their voices, consents, meanings and worldviews are always already excluded.

CONCLUSION

Ota Benga, Jean de Charles Menezes, Abeer Qassim Hamza al-Janabi and millions of others are always already dead within the world of international relations. Their voices, consents, and worldviews do not go into the making of the core concepts of IR. Their difference does not make a difference to our theorizations and imaginations of world politics. Isn't it this impoverishment that is implicit in the recognition that "IR is an American social science?"

Their bodies are already "fixed" within our colonial imaginaries in terms of the range of meanings they can carry and the emotions they can evoke.

Ota Benga = curiosity; Manei Shaman Turki al-Habadi, Yasser Talal al-Zahrani, Ali Abdullah Ahmed, Jamil el Banna = suspicion; Jean de Charles Menezes = suspicion because of a proximity to suspicious bodies; Abeer Qassim Hamza al-Janabi = pleasure.

If our feelings of curiosity, suspicion or pleasure are disrupted by the abrupt emergence or visibility of alternative narratives and of other worlds, we are stretched from "laws," "patterns" and "structures" towards "outliers" and "contingencies," from "interests" and "purposes" to "passions," "tragedies" and "compassion." Don't push us too far though. We might get tired—"compassion fatigue," "atrocity fatigue," as there is only so much any decent, normal, well-meaning human being can take. The world can be a depressing place

161

and, of course, we are all subject to the laws of diminishing marginal utility, there being only so many animals you can see and chicken wings you can enjoy.

It takes only a few deaths on our side to make an event, generate a crisis that can stop time, reconfigure space, turn local issues into global ones, produce a before and after, redraw boundaries and borders in theory and practice, everywhere and anywhere, around our loss and our pain. But hundreds of thousands of bodies on the side of the other barely disrupt the world of IR theory and practice. Should we be surprised?

Isn't it because Ota Benga, Jean de Charles Menezes, Abeer Qassim Hamza al-Janabi and millions of others are always already dead within the world of IR that their deaths don't raise a stink? These bodies cannot decompose, cannot rot, cannot raise a stench, cannot transform theory or practice, because they were never meaningfully alive within our zoological and museological modalities[1] and institutions. One can dissect these bodies, display them in precise and intricate ways, deploy sophisticated techniques to analyze them, intervene humanely on them, precisely because they have already been fixed, preserved, "plastinated,"[2] contained, quite rigorously. They can be stuffed, exhibited, treasured, studied, explored, admired, written about, circulated and disseminated among ourselves. But because they were never meaningfully alive, or alive in meaningful ways to us, because they have never been seen as making a difference to our lives, their deaths, conceptually and theoretically foretold, cannot be occasions for our mourning, for our weeping, for our shame or anger or rage or for any serious detraction, extrusion or loss of the self. Their deaths are academic and maybe "humanitarian" issues, but they are not human ones.

That is the IR I seem to be engaged to. It is an elegant and young social science. Others don't wither it. Their worlds don't transform it. Their deaths don't make it stink.

It is a world in which I can enter the classroom and ritually intone:

Welcome to "An Introduction to International Relations"!

Today, we will talk about power, a core concept in IR, and its many faces.

The first face of power involves "the ability of A to get B to do something that B would otherwise not do...."

As these words stumble out,

I will ask, give and get neat and clean examples.

I will compare and contrast and talk about the conceptual and analytical limitations of each of these faces.

I will generate analytical wonder by posing conceptual puzzles and then resolving them through technically sophisticated methods.

I will quiz and test them on their grasp of these fundamentals.

And all the while, as I do this, the face, voice, sentences and screams of Abeer Qassim Hamza al-Janabi, fourteen, and her family, will haunt me and mock my efforts.

She knows, they know, as I do, the number of ways in which I am lying.

She knows, they know, as I do, that neither my teaching nor my chosen discipline is currently in a position to do justice to their life and/or death or the worlds she and her family share with me.

She knows, they know, as I cannot bear to know, that today, I will be helping to make and remake the spaces, the fields, the houses of theory and practice, in which she and her family (and some/many parts of me) will be killed, again and again.

Mumbling to myself about the stress of a career in academia, of the relentless pressure to generate a decent body of published materials, reminding myself of the trauma of getting tenure and of retaining a job in a competitive and combative field, bolstering my cowardice/courage with horror stories of those who failed, I plead my helplessness and, therefore, I believe, my innocence.

I calm down. After the class ends, I go to the Main Building, to Calvin in The Retreat, and ask for a Philly Chicken Steak with a side order of chicken wings. Some El Diablo sauce on the side, please!

It's only 10.30 in the morning, a little early for lunch. But teaching IR theory, I have realized, makes me mindlessly hungry.

NOTES

INTRODUCTION

1. Suicide note by Jumah Abdel Latif al-Dossary, a prisoner at Guantanamo Bay; cited in Mahvish Khan, *My Guantanamo Diary: The Detainees and the Stories They Told Me*, New York: Public Affairs, 2008, p. 12.
2. Shashi Tharoor, "Make the world safe for diversity," *The Hindu*, 30 July 2006. Available at: http://www.hindu.com/mag/2006/07/30/stories/2006073000150300.htm; Accessed 14 May 2011.
3. Jenny Edkins, *Trauma and the Memory of Politics*, Cambridge: Cambridge University Press, 2003.
4. Ibid.
5. Dipesh Chakrabarty, *Provincializing Europe: Postcolonial Thought and Historical Difference*, Princeton: Princeton University Press, 2000.

1. SHAME AND RAGE

1. An earlier version of Chapter One appears in Robin Riley and Naeem Inayatullah (eds), *Interrogating Imperialism: Conversations on Gender, Race and War*, Palgrave Macmillan, 2006. Himadeep Muppidi, "Shame and Rage: International Relations and the World School of Colonialism" in Naeem Inayatullah and Robin Riley (edited), *Interrogating Imperialism: Conversations on Gender, Race and War*, 2006, Palgrave Macmillan. Reproduced with permission of Palgrave Macmillan.

2. See Abdelrahman Munif, *Cities of Salt*, New York: Vintage, 1989.

3. Adam Hochschild, *King Leopold's Ghost*, New York: Mariner's Books, 1998.

4. Ibid.

5. Royal Museum of Central Africa, *The Museum Key: A Visitor's Guide to the RMCA*, Tervuren, Belgium: RMCA, 2003, p. 81

6. Hochschild, *King Leopold's Ghost*, p. 276

7. "In this park we are building a museum that will be worthy of containing all these fine collections, and that will, I hope, effectively contribute to the colonial education of my countrymen." King Leopold II in conversation with the French architect Charles Girault, 1903. Quoted in *The Museum Key: A Vistor's Guide to the RMCA*, 2003, p. 78.

8. Hochschild, *King Leopold's Ghost*, p. 37

9. See UNESCO's World Heritage List, Grand-Place, Brussels (Belgium), No. 857, Advisory Body Evaluation, pp. 67–70. Document available online at http://whc.unesco.org/pg.cfm?cid=31&id_site=857

10. Ibid., p. 68.

11. Hochschild, *King Leopold's Ghost*.

12. Marcella Bombardieri, "Veterans of Iraq war join forces to protest US invasion," *Boston Globe*, 2 Sep. 2004. Accessed 25 May 2009 at http://www.boston.com/news/nation/articles/2004/09/02/veterans_of_iraq_war_join_forces_to_protest_us_invasion/

13. Amitav Ghosh, *In an Antique Land: History in the Guise of a Traveler's Tale*, New York: Vintage, 1992, p. 237

14. Ghosh, *In An Antique Land*, p. 236

15. Adam Gorlick, "Marine returns from Iraq to emotional ruin, suicide," Associated Press, *Boston Herald*, 16 Oct. 2004.

16. Ibid.

17. Lizette Alvarez, "Suicides of Soldiers Reach High of Nearly 3 Decades," *New York Times*, 30 Jan. 2009.

18. http://abcnews.go.com/WN/Politics/Story?id=6356046&page=3.

2. NUMB AND NUMBER

1. Juan Cole, *Cheney's Mission Accomplished*, Informed Comment, Blog, 17 Mar. 2009.
2. Ibid.
3. Steven Lee Myers and Alissa J. Rubin, "Iraqi Journalist Hurls Shoes at Bush and Denounces Him on TV as a 'Dog,' *New York Times*, 14 Dec. 2008. http://www.nytimes.com/2008/12/15/world/middleeast/15prexy.html
4. Ibid.
5. See, among others, Liz Sly, "Iraqi shoe-thrower goes on trial," www.chicagotribune.com, 19 Feb. 2009. Accessed 29 May 2009 at http://archives.chicagotribune.com/2009/feb/19/local/chi-iraq-shoe-thrower-090219
6. "Iraq court jails Bush shoe-thrower for three years," 12 Mar. 2009, http://www.google.com/hostednews/afp/article/ALeqM5i2JpIx2rJGrUhQVecW20yn8_dOAg
7. See, among others, Tawfeeq, Mohammed, and Jomana Karadsheh, "Monument to Bush shoe-throwing shines at Iraqi orphanage," 29 Jan. 2009, CNN Report. http://www.cnn.com/2009/WORLD/meast/01/29/iraq.shoe.monument/index.html
8. Commenting on these exit interviews given by President Bush and comparing them in tone and content with those given by Vice President Cheney, the *New York Times* noted that Bush appeared to be more interested in shaping "the views of historians" who would be writing about his Presidency. See Sheryl Gay Stolberg, "White House Views on Past 8 Years Diverge," *New York Times*, 24 Dec. 2008.
9. Myers and Rubin, "Iraqi Journalist Hurls Shoes at Bush and Denounces Him on TV as a 'Dog.'"
10. "Bush 'Not Insulted' by Thrown Shoes," President Talks With Martha Raddatz About Iraq and His Legacy, http://abcnews.go.com/Politics/BushLegacy/story?id=6460837&page=1
11. Roger Cohen, "Two Shoes for Democracy," *New York Times*, 22 Dec. 2008. http://www.nytimes.com/2008/12/22/opinion/22cohen.html
12. Ibid.

13. Barack Hussein Obama, Inaugural Speech, 20 Jan. 2009. Accessed 29 May 2009 at http://www.nytimes.com/2009/01/20/us/politics/20text-obama.html.

14. David Brown, "Study Claims Iraq's 'Excess' Death Toll Has Reached 655,000," *The Washington Post*, 11 Oct. 2006 p. A12. Accessed 29 May 2009 at http://www.washingtonpost.com/wpdyn/content/article/2006/10/10/AR2006101001442.html

15. James Carroll, "The Nagasaki Principle," *The Boston Globe*, 7 Aug. 2006. Accessed 8 July 2006 at http://www.commondreams.org/cgibin/print.cgi?file=/views06/0807-

16. Lawrence Freedman, *The Evolution of Nuclear Strategy*, New York: St. Martin's Press, 1981, p. 16. My emphasis.

17. Ibid., pp. 18–19. My emphasis.

18. Freedman, *The Evolution of Nuclear Strategy*, p. 19. Freedman's quotation of Stimson is footnoted as Henry L. Stimson and McGeorge Bundy, *On Active Service in Peace and War*, London, Hutchinson, 1948, pp. 36, 369–70, 373.

19. Freedman, *The Evolution of Nuclear Strategy*, p. 19. Freedman's quotation of General Marshall is footnoted to L. Giovannitti and F. Freed, *The Decision to Drop the Bomb*, London, Methuen & Co., 1967, p. 35.

20. Jim VandeHei and Robin Wright, "Bush says America will lead global relief effort," *The Washington Post*, 30 Dec. 2004, p.AO1.

21. "Condi Rice: Tsunami provided 'wonderful opportunity' for US," *Agence France Press*, 18 Jan. 2005.

22. Anne Gearan, "Powell: Tsunami aid may help fight terror," *Boston.com*, 4 Jan. 2005.

23. Arjun Appadurai, *Modernity at Large: Cultural Dimensions of Globalization*, Minneapolis: University of Minnesota Press, 1996.

24. Ibid., p. 125

25. Hergé, *The Adventures of Tintin Reporter for "Le Petit Vingtieme" in the Congo* (translated by Leslie Lonsdale-Cooper and Michael Turner), San Francisco, Last Gasp of San Francisco, 2002. Pages not numbered.

26. Ibid.

27. Johannes Fabian, *Time and the Other: How Anthropology Makes Its Object*, New York: Columbia University Press, 1983; Walter Mignolo, *The Darker Side of the Renaissance: Literacy, Territoriality, & Colonization*, 2nd Edition, Ann Arbor: University of Michigan Press, 2003; and Dipesh Chakrabarty, *Provincializing Europe: Postcolonial Thought and Historical Difference*, Princeton: Princeton University Press, 2000.

28. Hergé, *The Adventures of Tintin: Tintin in the Congo* (translated by Leslie Lonsdale-Cooper and Michael Turner), London, Egmont Books, 2005, pp. 36–37.

29. James William Gibson, *The Perfect War: Technowar in Vietnam*, New York: Atlantic Monthly Press, 1986; Phillip Carter, "How They Count the Enemy Dead: Why's it so hard? Let us count the ways," 17 Nov. 2004. Accessed 25 May 2009 at http://slate.com/toolbar.aspx?action=print&id=2109871

30. *USA Today*, October 2003. Accessed 17 May 2011 at http://www.usatoday.com/news/washington/executive/rumsfeld-memo.htm.

31. U.S. Department of Defense, Office of the Assistant Secretary of Defense (Public Affairs), News Transcript, Presenter: Colonel Michael Regner, Operations Officer, I Marine Expeditionary Force (G-3, I MEF), Monday, 15 Nov. 2004. Accessed 12 Feb. 2005 at http://www.dod.mil/cgi-bin/dlprint.cgi?http://www.dod.mil/transcripts/2004/tr20041115–1602.html; emphasis added.

32. Gibson, *The Perfect War*, p. 121

33. Richard T. Cooper, "General Casts War in Religious Terms," *Los Angeles Times*, 16 Oct. 2003. Accessed 13 Feb. 2005 at http://www.commondreams.org/cgi-bin/print.cgi?file=/headlines03/10

34. Esther Schrader, "General Draws Fire for Saying 'It's Fun to Shoot' the Enemy," *Los Angeles Times*, 4 Feb. 2005. Accessed 12 Feb. 2005 at http://www.commondreams.org/cgi-bin/print.cgi?file=/headlines05/02

35. Ibid.

36. I would argue that though there are many similarities between the modes of administering the historical colonial state and contemporary colonial discourses, there is also an important difference. A crucial distinction between the historical situation of European

colonialism and the contemporary one has to do with the emergence and acknowledgement of multiple "loci of enunciation" (Mignolo, *The Darker Side of the Renaissance*) within the contemporary spatio-temporal order. Colonialism in its earlier phase operated in a space where "global knowledge" or knowledge of "international relations" was hierarchically divided between an enlightened and knowing Europe/West and a seemingly benighted and unknowing rest. It was enough then for the colonizers to converse among themselves about themselves, and about others, and to venture to teach others about themselves. Decolonization, however, upset that hierarchy by empowering through statist and non-statist channels multiple loci of enunciation in the international system. While asymmetries in economic and military power undoubtedly persist, the world has essentially been, for quite some time now, multipolar in terms of the generation of understandings of itself. That poses new problems for a colonial imaginary not least of which is that number, by establishing a relationship of intersubjectivity, allows for the possibility of shared resistance.

37. See, for example, Mike Davis,, *Late Victorian Holocausts: El Niño Famines and the Making of the Third World*, New York: Verso, 2001; Adam Hochschild, *King Leopold's Ghost*; Tzvetan Todorov, *The Conquest of America: The Question of the Other*, Oklahoma University Press, 1999; Eduardo Galeano, *Memory of Fire*, Translated by Cedric Belfrage, London: Quartet Books, 1985, 1987 and 1989. First published as a single volume in 1995; and Walter Mignolo, *The Darker Side of the Renaissance*.

38. James Carroll, "The Nagasaki Principle," *The Boston Globe*, 7 Aug. 2006. Accessed 8 July 2006 at http://www.commondreams.org/cgibin/print.cgi?file=/views06/0807-

39. Gibson, *The Perfect War*, p. 319 (emphasis in original).

40. Graham Allison, "Lessons of Nagasaki for fighting terrorism," *The Boston Globe*, 9 Aug. 2004. Accessed 17 May 2011 at http://www.boston.com/news/globe/editorial_opinion/oped/articles/2004/08/09/lessons_of_nagasaki_for_fighting_terrorism/

41. Ibid. Emphasis added.

42. Hochschild, *King Leopold's Ghost*, and Hochschild, *Bury the*

Chains: Prophets and Rebels in the Fight to Free an Empire's Slaves, New York: Houghton Mifflin, 2005.

43. Adam Hochschild, "The idea that brought slavery to its knees," *The Los Angeles Times*, 25 Jan. 2005. Accessed 17 May 2011 at http://www.commondreams.org/views05/0125-27.htm.

44. Ibid.

45. Ibid.

46. Hochschild would probably know that by 1838, when he says that the Abolitionists finally succeeded, the British colonization of India was already on its way to lasting another 100 years at least. What then is the politics of constantly valorizing human rights and their heroes when the overall structure of colonial exploitation moves so seamlessly from one configuration to another?

47. Obama, "Inaugural Address."

48. Jean-Paul Sartre, Preface, in Frantz Fanon, *The Wretched of the Earth*, Paris, Maspero, 1961. Reproduced in Jean-Paul Sartre, *Colonialism and Neo-Colonialism* (translated by Azzedine Haddour, Steve Brewer and Terry McWilliams), New York, Routledge, 2001, p. 136.

49. Appadurai, *Modernity at Large*, pp. 125–6 (emphasis in original).

50. Dipesh Chakrabarty, *Provincializing Europe: Postcolonial Thought and Historical Difference*, Princeton: Princeton University Press, 2000; pp. 89–90.

51. I do not intend to belabor the point that international relations theory, as it is currently constituted, is far from achieving that task. That it is focused predominantly on reading and translating the global in and through a Western, frequently colonial and necessarily provincial, imaginary. Others have made that case quite well. See, for example, Naeem Inayatullah and David Blaney, *International Relations and the Problem of Difference*, New York: Routledge, 2004.

52. Ewan MacAskill, "President orders air strikes on villages in tribal area," *The Guardian*, 24 Jan. 2009.

53. See "Shoe-throwing monument removed from Iraqi orphanage," CNN, 30 Jan. 2009. Accessed 29 May 2009 at http://www.cnn.com/2009/WORLD/meast/01/30/iraq.shoe.monument/

54. John Dickerson, "The New Commander: James Mattis will replace David Petraeus as the commander of Centcom," http://www.slate.com/id/2258660.

55. Thom Shanker, "Petraeus's Successor is Known for Impolitic Words," *New York Times*, 19 July 2010. http://www.nytimes.com/2010/07/20/world/20mattis.html?scp=2&sq=mattis&st=cse.

3. PROPRIETY AND ATROCITY

1. George Monbiot, "The Turks haven't learned the British way of denying past atrocities," *The Guardian*, 27 Dec. 2005. Accessed 29 Dec. 2005 at http://www.guardian.co.uk/print/0,3858,53630 26–103390,00.html

2. Davis, *Late Victorian Holocausts*.

3. Caroline Elkins, *Imperial Reckoning: The Untold Story of Britain's Gulag in Kenya*, Owl Books, Henry Holt, 2005.

4. If a state can show its "brutality" to be non-anachronistic, to be somehow in "keeping with the times," and can argue that its violence is/was reasonable or sensible within a certain context, then it has access to a key form of power in the international system: the power to have its atrocities forgotten (foremost by the self). That is, the effective success of some states in erasing their atrocities from public/international and personal memory is intimately related to their capacity to embed those atrocities within categories/categorical structures presented as "rational" and in keeping with the times. Conversely, a "failed state" is, first and foremost, a failure in terms of its narrative abilities, in terms of its capacity to translate and account for its actions through categories that appear "sensible," "reasonable" and non-anachronistic within the dominant discourse.

5. Control over the interpretation of events, then, is a crucial form of state power. This in itself is not a novel insight. What is critical to examine is how this control is reproduced and sustained in the face of a changing world? In other words, the fact that explanations/interpretations have to be "non-anachronistic" or in keeping with the times gives a dynamic character to the mechanisms of interpretive power. Power that is effective is a power that knows how to keep its interpretations in tune with the times. This means a capac-

ity to adjust, to tweak, to revise, the readings of past events to bring them into line with current sensibilities in one way or another. Translation is key to this power. The translation of the self, of the actions of the self, to accommodate them to whatever the sensibilities of the present demand.

6. Niall Ferguson, *Empire: The Rise and Demise of the British World Order and the Lessons for Global Power*, New York: Basic Books, 2003, p. 152

7. Ibid., p. 152.

8. Ibid.

9. In separating good imperialists from worse ones, Ferguson also creates an internal hierarchy of imperialism within which British imperialism is portrayed as distinct from German and Belgian imperialisms. The mark of the good imperialist is stretched far enough for Ferguson to lay claim to an anti-imperialist heritage for imperial Britain. Ferguson does this by, first, drawing on Hochschild (*King Leopold's Ghost*) to argue that it was two "Britons" (Roger Casement and Edward Morel) who brought to light some of the Belgian atrocities in the Congo. Second, he claims that the British Empire had to break up and withdraw from its imperial enterprise not because of resistance from its colonies and subject peoples but because it expended itself and its empire in order to fight against various unjust imperialisms. Thus British colonialism was not only good by virtue of it being British but it also sacrificed itself in order to save subject peoples from other, "evil," forms of colonialism. (This is the heritage that he then nobly passes on to the US when he calls it an "anti-imperialist imperialist.")

10. The hierarchy he has established between the character of the British nation and that of others such as the Germans or (subsequently) the Japanese and the Russians also allows him to judge who would be a worthy successor to the British. Who would be the best inheritor of this mantle of good imperialist in the contemporary international system? Why, of course, the US! The US becomes the new "anti-imperialist imperialist" whose only problem, according to Ferguson, is its denial about its imperial identity.

11. In Peter Paret (ed.), *Makers of Modern Strategy: from Machiavelli to the Nuclear Age*, Princeton: Princeton University Press, 1986, pp. 380–81.

12. Assia Djebar, *Fantasia: An Algerian Cavalcade*, Translated by Dorothy S. Blair, Portsmouth, NH: Heinemann, 1993, pp. 64–79.

13. My reading of the original article by Melvin Richter on which this claim is based leads to a different interpretation. Melvin Richter's article, contrary to Porch's claim here, is an analysis and direct indictment of Tocqueville's silence on many of these atrocities and his overall support for French policy in Algeria. See Melvin Richter, "Tocqueville on Algeria," *The Review of Politics*, 25:3, July 1963, pp. 362–398. Like Ferguson, who forgets to mention the Irish nationalism motivating Roger Casement, a nationalism that some have argued actually makes it possible for him to relate to and see Belgian colonization from the African side (Hochschild, *King Leopold's Ghost*), Porch appears to be in a hurry to produce condemnation from within.

14. Howard Kurtz, "CNN Chief Orders 'Balance' in War News; Reporters are told to remind viewers why U.S. is bombing," *The Washington Post*, 31 Oct. 2001, pg. C.01.

15. Ibid. Accessed 17 May 2011 at http://www.washingtonpost.com/ac2/wp-dyn?pagename= article&contentId=A14435–2001Oct30.

16. Ibid.

17. When asked if this information wasn't already available to the "viewers who don't live in caves," Isaacson said, "People do already know it." "We go to Ground Zero all the time. We cover the memorial services. We cover people's lives that have been touched. I just want to make sure we keep a sense of balance." Kurtz, "CNN Chief Orders 'Balance' in War News; Reporters are told to remind viewers why U.S. is bombing."

4. ZOOLOGICAL RELATIONS

1. An earlier version of this chapter is in Andrew Davison and Himadeep Muppidi (eds), *Europe and its Boundaries: Words and Worlds, Within and Beyond*, Lanham, MD: Lexington Books, 2009. Himadeep Muppidi, "Zoological Relations," in Andrew Davison and Himadeep Muppidi (edited), *Europe and Its Boundaries: Words and Worlds, Within and Beyond*, 2009, Lexington Books. Reproduced with permission of Lexington Books.

2. "Verbatim," TIME, 9 July 2007, p. 10.

3. "If I Ran the Zoo," 1950, renewed 1977 by Dr. Seuss Enterprises. From *A Hatful of Seuss: Five Favorite Dr. Seuss Stories*, New York: Random House, 1997, pp. 96–97.

4. Ibid.

5. Ibid.

6. Mitch Keller, "The Scandal at the Zoo," *New York Times*, 6 Aug. 2006. Accessed 7 May 2009 at http://www.nytimes.com/2006/08/06/nyregion/thecity/06zoo.html

7. Ibid.

8. Ibid.

9. Ibid.

10. Ibid.

11. Sabrina Tavernise, "Civilians Lose as Fighters Slip Into Fog of War," *New York Times*, 3 Aug. 2006. Accessed 7 May 2009 at http://www.nytimes.com/2006/08/03/world/middleeast/03civilian.html?fta=y.

12. "I saw Tube man shot—eyewitness," BBC News. http://news.bbc.co.uk/1/hi/uk/4706913.stm. Accessed 7 May 2009.

13. Ibid.

14. Alastair Jamieson and Craig Brown, "Blunders led to police killing of an innocent man," *The Scotsman*, 17 Aug. 2005. Accessed 7 May 2009 at http://thescotsman.scotsman.com/latestnews/Blunders-led-to-police-killing.2652700.jp

15. Admiral Harry B. Harris, Jr., "Inside Guantanamo Bay," *Chicago Tribune*, 17 May 2006.

16. Suzanne Goldberg and Hugh Muir, "Killing themselves was unnecessary. But it certainly is a good PR move," *The Guardian*, 12 June 2006. Accessed 7 May 2009 at http://www.guardian.co.uk/world/2006/jun/12/guantanamo.topstories3

17. Ibid.

18. "If I Ran the Zoo," from *A Hatful of Seuss*.

19. *Hobson-Jobson: The Anglo-Indian Dictionary: A spice-box of etymological curiosities and colourful expressions*, 1886, pp. 595, 329, 750 respectively.

20. From *Encarta World English Dictionary*, New York: St. Martins Press, 1999, p. 1187.

21. Diane Taylor, "I miss my dad so much," *The Guardian*, 18 Mar. 2006. Accessed 7 May 2009 at http://www.guardian.co.uk/life-andstyle/2006/mar/18/familyandrelationships.family3

22. Ibid.

23. Ibid.

24. Ibid.

25. *Guide Antwerp Zoo*, p. 5.

26. *Guide Antwerp Zoo*, Rudy Van Eysendeyk, General Director, "Welcome to the Antwerp Zoo."

27. Ibid.

28. *Zoo Tracks, Minnesota Zoo: Changing how you see the world*, July/Aug. 2007, p. 9.

29. "Global domination via the back door," *The Financial Times*, 10 June 2008, p. 10.

30. "San Diego Zoo: It's a jungle in here," Brochure, 2005.

31. *Como Park Zoo and Conservatory: Invest in a Treasured Resource*, Brochure.

32. Bill Allen, "From the Editor," *National Geographic*, Vol. 201, Issue 4; April 2002; Also, Cathy Newman and Steve McCurry, "A Life Revealed," *National Geographic*, April 2002.

33. Ibid.

34. Ibid.

35. Cathy Newman and Steve McCurry, "A Life Revealed," *National Geographic*, April 2002.

36. Ibid.

37. Bernard Cohn, *Colonialism and Its Forms of Knowledge*, Princeton University Press, 1996, p. 86.

38. Cathy Newman and Steve McCurry, "A Life Revealed."

39. Ibid.

40. Ibid.

41. Ibid.

42. Ibid.

43. *Guide Antwerp Zoo*, p. 42.

5. HUMANITARIANISM AND ITS VIOLENCES

1. Raymond D. Duvall, Morse-Alumni Distinguished Teaching Professor and Chair, Department of Political Science, University of Minnesota, Minneapolis.

2. I would like to thank, without implicating them in this argument, Andy Davison and Michael Barnett for very helpful comments, suggestions and criticisms.

3. David Rieff, *A Bed for the Night: Humanitarianism in Crisis*, New York: Simon & Schuster, 2002, p. 33

4. Ibid.

5. Ibid., p. 53

6. Ibid., p. 36

7. See MSF website, accessed 4 June 2004 at http://www.msf.org.hk/public/contents/news?ha=&wc=0&hb=&hc=&revision_id=5236&item_id=5235

8. Hugo Slim, "Politicizing Humanitarian Action According to Need," Presentation to the 2nd International Meeting on Good Humanitarian Donorship, Ottawa, 21–22 Oct. 2004, p. 2.

9. Tzvetan Todorov, *The Conquest of America: The Question of the Other*, Oklahoma: Oklahoma University Press, 1999, p. 169.

10. Rieff, *A Bed For the Night*.

11. David Kennedy, *The Dark Sides of Virtue*, Princeton: Princeton University Press, 2005.

12. Rieff, *A Bed For the Night*, pp. 257–258.

13. Kennedy, *The Dark Sides of Virtue*, pp. xxiv-xxvi

14. Fanon, *The Wretched of the Earth*, p. 6

15. Ibid., p. 37

16. Ibid., p. 40.

6. POSTCOLONIALITY AND INTERNATIONAL POLITICAL ECONOMY

1. I would like to thank Andy Davison and Chris Chekuri for critical comments on various versions of this chapter.

2. Thomas Friedman, *The World is Flat*, New York: Farrar, Straus & Giroux, 2005.

3. Thomas Friedman, *The Lexus and the Olive Tree*, New York: Farrar, Straus & Giroux, 2000.

4. Thomas Friedman, *The World is Flat*, pp. 185–191

5. James Hevia, *English Lessons: The Pedagogy of Imperialism in Nineteenth-Century China*, Durham: Duke University Press, 2003.

6. Benjamin J. Cohen, "The transatlantic divide: Why are American and British IPE so different?" *Review of International Political Economy*, 14:2, May 2007, pp. 197–219.

7. Ibid.

8. Benjamin Cohen, *International Political Economy: An Intellectual History*, Princeton: Princeton University Press, 2008.

9. Richard Higgott and Matthew Watson, "All at sea in a barbed wire canoe: Professor Cohen's transatlantic voyage in IPE," *Review of International Political Economy*, 15:1, Feb. 2008, pp. 1–17.

10. John Ravenhill, "In search of the missing middle," *Review of International Political Economy*, 15:1, Feb. 2008, pp. 18–29.

11. Cohen, "The transatlantic divide," p. 198.

12. Jan Nederveen Pieterse, "Political and Economic Brinksmanship," *Review of International Political Economy*, 14:3, 2007, pp. 467–486.

13. Mahmood Mamdani, "The Politics of Naming: Genocide, Civil War, Insurgency," *London Review of Books*, 8 Mar. 2007. Available at http://www.lrb.co.uk/v29/n05/mamd01.html

14. Craig Whitlock and Shannon Smiley, "Non-European PhDs in Germany Find Use of 'Doktor' Verboten," *The Washington Post*, Friday, 14 Mar. 2008; Page A01.

15. Ibid.

16. See the *New York Times* editorial on Tata's production of a $2000 car, the Nano. Accessed 29 May 2009 at http://www.nytimes.com/2008/01/16/opinion/16wed4.html

17. See ABC story on "Marines and Operation Baghdad Pups," accessed 29 May 2009 at http://abclocal.go.com/wpvi/story?section=news/special_reports&id=6115518

18. Faiq, ABC News, 21 Mar. 2008; Tom Englehardt (2008), TomDispatch.com; "What Price Slaughter? In New York and Jalalabad, Human Life Is Valued Differently—by the US Government."

19. Hochschild, *King Leopold's Ghost*.

20. Philippe Naughton, "Puppy-toss video makes Marine figure of hate," www.thetimes.co.uk, 4 Mar. 2008. Accessed 28 May 2009 at http://www.timesonline.co.uk/tol/news/world/iraq/article3481977.ece

7. COGNITION AND COMPLICITY

1. Todd S. Purdum, "Across US, Outrage at Response," *New York Times*, 3 Sep. 2005. http://www.nytimes.com/2005/09/03/national/nationalspecial/03voices.html?pagewanted=print

2. Ceci Connolly, "Frustration Grows In Days Stranded On Interstate 10," *The Washington Post*, 3 Sep. 2005; p. A13.

3. William Safire, "Katrina Words," *New York Times*, 18 Sep. 2005. Also, National Public Radio (NPR), "On the Media: Word Watch: Refugees," 9 Sep. 2005, WNYC Radio. www.onthemedia.org/transcripts/transcripts_090905_refugee.html

4. NPR, "On The Media, Word Watch: Refugees," 9 Sept. 2005. Transcript available at http://www.onthemedia.org/yore/transcripts/transcripts_090905_refugee.html, accessed 17 May 2011.

5. Encarta World English Dictionary, New York: St. Martin's Press, 1999.

6. NPR, "On The Media, Word Watch: Refugees."

7. Rev. Jesse Jackson, Speech to the Transport Workers Union of America's 22nd Constitutional Convention, 20 Sep. 2005. Accessed 19 Dec. 2005 at http://www.twu.org/homeindex/convention/jackson.html

8. NPR, "On The Media, Word Watch: Refugees."

9. Tim Craig and Michael D. Shear, "Allen Quip Provokes Outrage, Apology," *The Washington Post*, washingtonpost.com, Tuesday, 15 Aug. 2006, A01. Accessed 24 Aug. 2006 at http://www.washingtonpost.com/wp-dyn/content/article/2006/08/14/

10. Ibid.

11. Ibid.

12. Wikipedia, "Macaca." Originally accessed 2006, accessed again 17 May 2011 at http://en.wikipedia.org/wiki/Macaca_%28slur%29

13. Ibid.

14. Robert B. Edgerton, *The Troubled Heart of Africa: A History of the Congo*, St. Martin's Press, New York, pp. 180–181, 184. Cited in Wikipedia, "Macaca."

15. Robin Morgan, "Their Bodies as Weapons," *The Guardian*, 21 Aug. 2006. Accessed 24 Aug. 2006 at http://www.commondreams.org/cgi-bin/print.cgi?file=/views06/0821

16. Ibid.
17. Ibid.

CONCLUSION

1. Bernard Cohn, *Colonialism and Its Forms of Knowledge: The British in India*, Princeton: Princeton University Press, 1996.
2. Gunther Von Hagen's technique for preserving dead bodies.

BIBLIOGRAPHY

Agence France Press, "Condi Rice: Tsunami provided 'wonderful opportunity' for US," 18 Jan. 2005.

Allison, Graham, "Lessons of Nagasaki for Fighting Terrorism," *The Boston Globe*, 9 Aug. 2004. Accessed (8 Oct. 2004) from http://www.commondreams.org/views04/0809–07.htm

—— *Nuclear Terrorism: The Ultimate Preventable Catastrophe*, New York: New York Times Books, Henry Holt and Co., 2004.

Alvarez, Lizette, "Suicides of Soldiers Reach High of Nearly 3 Decades," *The New York Times*, 30 Jan. 2009.

Appadurai, Arjun, *Modernity at Large: Cultural Dimensions of Globalization*, Minneapolis: University of Minnesota Press, 1996.

Bombardieri, Marcella, "Veterans of Iraq war join forces to protest US invasion," *Boston Globe*, 2 Sep. 2004. Available online (accessed 25 May 2009) at: http://www.boston.com/news/nation/articles/2004/09/02/veterans_of_iraq_war_join_forces_to_protest_us_invasion/

Brown, David, "Study Claims Iraq's 'Excess' Death Toll Has Reached 655,000," *The Washington Post*, 11 Oct. 2006 p. A12. Accessed (29 May 2009) at:http://www.washingtonpost.com/wpdyn/content/article/2006/10/10/AR2006 101001442.html

Carroll, James, "The Nagasaki Principle," *The Boston Globe*, 7 Aug. 2006. Accessed (8 July 2006) http://www.commondreams.org/cgi-bin/print.cgi?file=/views06/0807-

Carter, Phillip, "How They Count the Enemy Dead: Why's it so hard? Let us count the ways," 17 Nov. 2004. Accessed (25 May 2009) http://slate.com/toolbar.aspx?action=print&id=2109871

BIBLIOGRAPHY

Chakrabarty, Dipesh, *Provincializing Europe: Postcolonial Thought and Historical Difference*, Princeton: Princeton University Press, 2000.

Cohen, Benjamin J., "The transatlantic divide: Why are American and British IPE so different?" *Review of International Political Economy*, 14:2, May 2007, pp. 197–219.

———— "The transatlantic divide: A rejoinder," *Review of International Political Economy*, 15:1, February 2008, pp. 30–34.

Cohen, Roger, "Two Shoes for Democracy," *New York Times*, 22 Dec. 2008. http://www.nytimes.com/2008/12/22/opinion/22cohen.html

Cohn, Bernard, *Colonialism and Its Forms of Knowledge: The British in India*, Princeton: Princeton University Press, 1996.

Cole, Juan, *Cheney's Mission Accomplished*, Informed Comment, Blog, 17 Mar. 2009.

Connolly, Ceci, "Frustration Grows In Days Stranded On Interstate 10," *The Washington Post*, 3 Sep. 2005; p. A13.

Cooper, Richard T., "General Casts War in Religious Terms," *The Los Angeles Times*, 16 Oct. 2003. Accessed (13 Feb. 2005) http://www.commondreams.org/cgi-bin/print.cgi?file=/headlines03/10

Craig, Tim, and Michael D. Shear, "Allen Quip Provokes Outrage, Apology," washingtonpost.com, Tuesday, 15 Aug. 2006, A01. Accessed 24 Aug. 2006 from: http://www.washingtonpost.com/wp-dyn/content/article/2006/08/14/

Crossen, Cynthia, "How Pygmy Ota Benga Ended Up in Bronx Zoo as Darwinism Dawned," *Wall Street Journal*, 6 Feb. 2006, pg. B. 1. Accessed (13 Mar. 2006) through: http://proquest.umi.com/pdweb?did=98186851&sid=4&Fmt=3&clientId=2641&RQT=309&VName=PQD

Davis, Mike, *Late Victorian Holocausts: El Niño Famines and the Making of the Third World*, New York: Verso, 2002.

Davison, Andrew and Himadeep Muppidi (eds), *Europe and its Boundaries: Words and Worlds, Within and Beyond*, Lanham, MD: Lexington Books, 2009.

Djebar, Assia, *Fantasia: An Algerian Cavalcade*, Translated by Dorothy S. Blair, Portsmouth, NH: Heinemann, 1993.

Edgerton, Robert B., *The Troubled Heart of Africa: A History of the Congo*, New York: St. Martin's Press, pp. 180–181,184.

BIBLIOGRAPHY

Edkins, Jenny, *Trauma and the Memory of Politics*, Cambridge: Cambridge University Press, 2003.

Elkins, Caroline, *Imperial Reckoning: The Untold Story of Britain's Gulag in Kenya*, New York: Owl Books, 2005.

Encarta World English Dictionary, New York: St. Martin's Press, 1999.

Englehardt, Tom, "Blowing Them Away Means Never Having to Say You're Sorry: Globalization Bush Style," 16 Mar. 2008, www.TomDispatch.com

——— "What Price Slaughter? In New York and Jalalabad, Human Life Is Valued Differently—by the U.S. Government." www.TomDispatch.com

Fabian, Johannes, *Time and the Other: How Anthropology Makes Its Object*, New York: Columbia University Press, 1983.

Faiq, Addel, "Blackwater 'Blood Money Angers Iraqis,'" ABC News, 21 Mar. 2008.

Fanon, Frantz, *The Wretched of the Earth*, Translated from the French by Richard Philcox, with commentary by Jean-Paul Sartre and Homi K. Bhabha, New York: Grove Press, 1963, 2004.

Ferguson, Niall, *Empire: The Rise and Demise of the British World Order and the Lessons for Global Power*, New York: Basic Books, 2003.

Freedman, Lawrence, *The Evolution of Nuclear Strategy*, New York: St. Martin's Press, 1981.

Friedman, Thomas, *The World is Flat*, New York: Farrar, Straus & Giroux, 2005.

——— *The Lexus and the Olive Tree*, New York: Farrar, Straus & Giroux, 2000.

Galeano, Eduardo, *Memory of Fire*, Translated by Cedric Belfrage, London: Quartet Books, 1985, 1987 and 1989. First published as a single volume in 1995.

Gearan, Anne, "Powell: Tsunami aid may help fight terror," *Boston.com*, 4 Jan. 2005.

Ghosh, Amitav, *In an Antique Land: History in the Guise of a Traveler's Tale*, New York: Vintage, 1992.

Gibson, James William, *The Perfect War: Technowar in Vietnam*, New York: Atlantic Monthly Press, 1986.

Goldenberg, Suzanne, and Hugh Muir, "Killing themselves was unnecessary. But it certainly is a good PR move," *The Guardian*,

12 Jun. 2006. Accessed (7 May 2009) at: http://www.guardian. co.uk/world/2006/jun/12/guantanamo.topstories3

Gorlick, Adam, "Marine returns from Iraq to emotional ruin, suicide," Associated Press, *Boston Herald*, 16 Oct. 2004.

Harris Jr., Harry B., "Inside Guantanamo Bay," *Chicago Tribune*, May 17, 2006, p. 27. Accessed (21 Aug. 2006) from http://proquest.umi.com.libproxy.vassar.edu/pqdweb?index=0&sid=2

Hergé, *The Adventures of Tintin: Tintin in the Congo*, Translated by Leslie Lonsdale-Cooper and Michael Turner, London: Egmont Books, 2005.

Hevia, James, *English Lessons: The Pedagogy of Imperialism in Nineteenth-Century China*, Durham: Duke University Press, 2003.

Higgott, Richard, and Matthew Watson, "All at sea in a barbed wire canoe: Professor Cohen's transatlantic voyage in IPE," *Review of International Political Economy*, 15:1, Feb. 2008, pp. 1–17.

Hochschild, Adam, *Bury the Chains: Prophets and Rebels in the Fight to Free an Empire's Slaves*, New York: Houghton Mifflin, 2005.

—— "The Idea That Brought Slavery to Its Knees," *Los Angeles Times*, 25 Jan. 2005, Accessed (19 Feb. 2005) from http://www.commondreams.org/cgi-bin/print.cgi?file=/views05/0125-

—— *King Leopold's Ghost*, New York: Mariner's Books, 1998.

Inayatullah, Naeem, and David Blaney, *International Relations and the Problem of Difference*, New York: Routledge, 2004.

Jackson, Rev. Jesse, Speech to the Transport Workers Union of America's 22nd Constitutional Convention, 20 Sep. 2005. Text accessed 19 Dec. 2005 from http://www.twu.org/homeindex/convention/jackson.html

Jamieson, Alastair, and Craig Brown, "Blunders led to police killing of an innocent man," *The Scotsman*, 17 Aug. 2005. Accessed (7 May 2009) at: http://thescotsman.scotsman.com/latestnews/Blunders-led-to-police-killing.2652700.jp

Keller, Mitch "The Scandal at the Zoo," *New York Times*, 6 Aug.2006, Accessed (7 May 2009) at http://www.nytimes.com/2006/08/06/nyregion/thecity/06zoo.html

Kennedy, David, *The Dark Sides of Virtue*, Princeton: Princeton University Press, 2005.

Khan, Mahvish, *My Guantanamo Diary: The Detainees and the Stories They Told Me*, New York: Public Affairs, 2008.

BIBLIOGRAPHY

Kurtz, Howard, "CNN Chief Orders 'Balance' in War News; Reporters are told to remind viewers why U.S. is bombing," *The Washington Post*, 31 Oct. 2001, pg. C.01.

MacAskill, Ewen, "President orders air strikes on villages in tribal area," *The Guardian*, 24 Jan. 2009.

Mamdani, Mahmood, *Good Muslim, Bad Muslim: America, the Cold War, and the Roots of Terror*, New York: Three Leaves Press, Doubleday, 2005.

——— "The Politics of Naming: Genocide, Civil War, Insurgency," *London Review of Books*, 8 Mar. 2007. Available at: http://www.lrb.co.uk/v29/n05/mamd01_.html

Mignolo, Walter, *The Darker Side of the Renaissance: Literacy, Territoriality, & Colonization, 2nd Edition*, Ann Arbor: University of Michigan Press, 2003.

Monbiot, George, "The Turks haven't learned the British way of denying past atrocities," *The Guardian*, 27 Dec. 2005. Accessed (29 Dec. 2005) from: http://www.guardian.co.uk/print/0,3858,5363026–103390,00.html

Morgan, Robin, "Their Bodies as Weapons," *The Guardian*, 21 Aug. 2006. Accessed (24 Aug. 2006) from: http://www.commondreams.org/cgi-bin/print.cgi?file=/views06/0821

Munif, AbdelRahman, *Cities of Salt*, New York: Vintage, 1989.

Myers, Steven Lee, and Alissa J. Rubin, "Iraqi Journalist Hurls Shoes at Bush and Denounces Him on TV as a 'Dog,'" *New York Times*, 14 Dec. 2008. http://www.nytimes.com/2008/12/15/world/middleeast/15prexy.html

Naughton, Philippe, "Puppy-toss video makes Marine figure of hate," www.thetimes.co.uk, 4 Mar. 2008. Accessed (28 May 2009) at: http://www.timesonline.co.uk/tol/news/world/iraq/article3481977.ece

Newman, Cathy, "A Life Revealed," *National Geographic*, April 2002.

Obama, Barack Hussein, Inaugural Speech, 20 January 2009. Available at http://www.nytimes.com/2009/01/20/us/politics/20text-obama.html (accessed 29 May 2009).

On the media from NPR, "Word Watch: Refugees," September 9, 2005, Accessed (19 Dec. 2005) from http://www.onthemedia.org/transcripts/transcripts_090905_refugee.html; Also accessed (25 May 2009) from: http://www.onthemedia.org/yore/transcripts/transcripts_090905_refugee.html

BIBLIOGRAPHY

Paret, Peter (ed.), *Makers of Modern Strategy: from Machiavelli to the Nuclear Age*, Princeton: Princeton University Press, 1986.

Pieterse, Jan Nederveen, "Political and Economic Brinksmanship," *Review of International Political Economy*, 14:3, 2007, pp. 467–486.

Porch, Douglas, "Bugeaud, Galliéni, Lyautey: The Development of French Colonial Warfare," in Paret, Peter (ed.), *Makers of Modern Strategy: from Machiavelli to the Nuclear Age*, Princeton: Princeton University Press, 1986, pp. 376–407.

Ravenhill, John, "In search of the missing middle," *Review of International Political Economy*, 15:1, February 2008, pp. 18–29.

Richter, Melvin, "Tocqueville on Algeria," *The Review of Politics*, 25:3, July 1963, pp. 362–398.

Rieff, David, *A Bed for the Night: Humanitarianism in Crisis*, New York: Simon & Schuster, 2002.

Riley, Robin, and Naeem Inayatullah (eds), *Interrogating Imperialism: Conversations on Gender, Race and War*, Palgrave Macmillan, 2006.

Royal Museum of Central Africa, *The Museum Key: A Visitor's Guide to the RMCA*, Tervuren, Belgium: RMCA, 2003.

Safire, William, "Katrina Words," *New York Times*, 18 Sep. 2005.

Schell, Jonathan, "Letter from Ground Zero: Something Strange," *The Nation*, 7 Jan. 2005. Accessed from http://www.commondreams.org/views05/0107-22.htm

Schrader, Esther, "General Draws Fire for Saying 'It's Fun to Shoot' the Enemy," *Los Angeles Times*, 4 Feb. 2005. Accessed (12 Feb. 2005) from http://www.commondreams.org/cgi-bin/print.cgi?file=/headlines05/02.

Dr. Seuss, *A Hatful of Seuss: Five Favorite Dr. Seuss Stories*, Random House: New York, 1997.

Slim, Hugo, "Politicizing Humanitarian Action According to Need," Presentation to the 2nd International Meeting on Good Humanitarian Donorship, Ottawa, 21–22 Oct. 2004.

Sly, Liz, "Iraqi shoe-thrower goes on trial," www.chicagotribune.com, 19 Feb. 2009, available (29 May 2009) at: http://archives.chicagotribune.com/2009/feb/19/local/chi-iraq-shoe-thrower-090219

Stolberg, Sheryl Gay, "White House Views on Past 8 Years Diverge," *New York Times*, 24 Dec. 2008.

Tannenwald, Nina, *The Nuclear Taboo: The United States and the Non-Use of Nuclear Weapons Since 1945*, Cambridge: Cambridge University Press, 2007.

Tavernise, Sabrina, "Civilians Lose as Fighters Slip Into Fog of War," *New York Times*, 3 Aug. 2006, accessed (7 May 2009) at http://www.nytimes.com/2006/08/03/world/middleeast/03civilian.html?fta=y

Tawfeeq, Mohammed, and Jomana Karadsheh, "Monument to Bush shoe-throwing shines at Iraqi orphanage," 29 Jan. 2009, CNN Report. http://www.cnn.com/2009/WORLD/meast/01/29/iraq.shoe.monument/index.ht ml

Taylor, Diane, "I miss my dad so much," *The Guardian*, 18 Mar. 2006. Accessed (22 Aug. 2006) from http://www.guardian.co.uk/print/0,329436615–111575,00.html

Tharoor, Shashi, "Make the world safe for diversity," *The Hindu*, 30 July 2006, available at: http://www.hindu.com/mag/2006/07/30/stories/2006073000150300.htm; accessed 14 May 2011

Todorov, Tzvetan, *The Conquest of America: The Question of the Other*, Oklahoma University Press, 1999.

U.S. Department of Defense, Office of the Assistant Secretary of Defense (Public Affairs), News Transcript, Presenter: Colonel Michael Regner, Operations Officer, I Marine Expeditionary Force (G-3, I MEF), Monday, 15 Nov. 2004. Available (accessed 12 Feb. 2005) at: http://www.dod.mil/cgi-bin/dlprint.cgi?http://www.dod.mil/transcripts/2004/tr20041115–1602.html; Also accessed 25 May 2009. http://www.defenselink.mil/transcripts/transcript.aspx?transcriptid=2157

VandeHei, Jim, and Robin Wright, "Bush says America will lead global relief effort," *The Washington Post*, 30 Dec. 2004, p.AO1.

Van Eysendeyk, R., *Guide Antwerp Zoo*, Antwerp, Belgium: Zoo Antwerp, 2005.

Whalley, Angelina (ed.), *Pushing the Limits: Encounters with Body Worlds Creator Gunther Von Hagens*, Heidelberg, Germany: Arts & Sciences, 2005.

Whitlock, Craig, and Shannon Smiley, "Non-European PhDs in Germany Find Use of 'Doktor' Verboten," *Washington Post*, Friday, 14 Mar. 2008; Page A01.

BIBLIOGRAPHY

Yule, Henry, and A.C. Burnell, *Hobson-Jobson: The Anglo-Indian Dictionary: A Spice Box of Etymological Curiosities and Colourful Expressions*, (First published 1886), Ware, Hertfordshire, U.K: Wordsworth Editions Ltd., 1996.

INDEX